WILD GEESE RETURN

WILD GEESE
RETURNING

CHINESE REVERSIBLE POEMS

By Michèle Métail

Translated by Jody Gladding
Introduction by Jeffrey Yang

THE CHINESE UNIVERSITY OF HONG KONG PRESS

NEW YORK REVIEW BOOKS

Calligrams
Series editor: Eliot Weinberger
Series designer: Leslie Miller

Wild Geese Returning: Chinese Reversible Poems
  By Michèle Métail
  Translated by Jody Gladding

By courtesy of Edition Tarabuste, France
Original 2011 French edition by Edition Tarabuste, France
Calligrams edition © 2017 by The Chinese University of Hong Kong
Introduction to the Calligrams edition © 2017 by Jeffrey Yang

A catalog record for this book is available from
the Library of Congress.

ISBN: 978-962-996-800-7
Available as an electronic book; ISBN: 978-962-996-816-8

Published by:

The Chinese University Press
The Chinese University of Hong Kong
Sha Tin, N.T., Hong Kong
www.chineseupress.com

New York Review Books
435 Hudson Street, New York, NY 10014, U.S.A.
www.nyrb.com

Printed in Hong Kong
10 9 8 7 6 5 4 3 2 1

Contents

Introduction to the Calligrams Edition   xiii

Introduction   xxxv

A Certain Predisposition in the Language   xxxix

Origins of the Reversible Poem   xlv

Period of the Six Dynasties (3rd to 6th centuries)

The Poem on a Tray   3

Su Hui: The Map of the Armillary Sphere   9

The Cosmological Foundations of the Poem   15

A Poem in Colors   23

Three Thousand One Hundred Twenty Poems   29

The Efficacy of the Form   53

The Poem between Heaven and Earth   67

From the Poem to the Legend   69

He Daoqing (5th century)   83

Wang Rong (468–494)   85

Yin Zhongkan (5th century)   89

The Xiao Court   91

Tang Dynasty (618–907)

Li Shimin: Emperor Taizong (599–649)   99

Anonymous: The Hermit of the South Mountains   101

Anonymous (7th century):
    The Map on a Hanging Mirror (*Panjiantu*)   105

Quan Deyu (759–818) and Pan Mengyang (?)   113

Lü Dongbin (798–?)   115

Pi Rixiu (834–883) and Lu Guimeng (?–881)   119

Song Dynasty (960–1279): Northern Song (960–1127) & Southern Song (1127–1279)

Xu Yin (Five Dynasties)   127

Qian Weizhi (942–1014)   129

Sun Mingfu (992–1057) and Pei Yu (?)   135

Mei Chuang (?)   143

Liu Chang (1019–1068)   151

Kong Pingzhong (11th century)   153

Wang Anshi (1021–1086)   159

Su Dongpo (1036–1101)   163

Qin Guan (1049–1100)   175

Yuwen Xuzhong (1079–1146)   179

Yang Wanli (1127–1206)   187

Zhu Xi (1130–1200)   189

Ming Dynasty (1368–1644)

Qiu Jun (1418/1421–1495)   193

Wang Shizhen (1526–1590)   197

Tang Xianzu (1550–1616)   199

Li Yang (?)   201

Cao Fengzu (?)   209

Qing Dynasty (1644–1911)

Wan Shu (1625–1688)   219

Zhang Yude (late 18th century)   223

Return to the West   235

Appendix: The Ways of Reading Su Hui's Poem   237

Selected Bibliography   261

Figures

1.1　The original form of Poem on a Tray　　6

1.2　Circular reading direction for Poem on a Tray　　6

1.3　Reconstruction of the words in Poem on a Tray　　7

2.1　Remains of a square poem in five colors　　14

3.1　The Armillary Sphere in Chinese cosmology　　15

3.2　Reproduction of the Armillary Sphere by Zhu Shuzhen　　16

3.3a　*Yin* and *Yang* lines from *The Book of Changes*　　18

3.3b　*Yin* and *Yang* combination lines from *The Book of Changes*　　18

3.4　Eight trigrams　　18

3.5　Sixty-four hexagrams　　20

4.1　The distribution of colors in the poem　　24

4.2　Replica of a Han Dynasty compass　　26

4.3　Northern Dipper or Big Dipper　　26

4.4　Map of the Armillary Sphere　　28

6.1　The Magic Square　　55

6.2　Eight Trigrams within the Magic Square　　56

6.3　Interaction of the *Yin* and the *Yang*　　58

6.4　The Sequence of Earlier Heaven　　58

6.5　Twelve Months Distributed around a Square　　60

6.6　Twenty-fourth hexagram from the *I Ching*　　61

6.7　Twenty-third hexagram from the *I Ching*　　62

6.8 Forty-third and Forty-fourth hexagrams from the *I Ching* 62

6.9 Taoist Cosmic Diagram 64

8.1 *Lady Su Hui and Her Verse Puzzle* 76

8.2 The Principle Female Role (Su Hui) 77

8.3 Reversible poems in an embroidered handkerchief 79

10.1 Wang Rong's Reversible Text 87

11.1 Reversible Inscription by Yin Zhongkan 89

12.1 Reversible Inscription by Xiao Yan 91

12.2 Reversible Inscription by Xiao Gang 91

13.1 Circular Text by Emperor Taizong 99

14.1 Square Arrangement of Text 101

14.2 Reading Order of the Square Arrangement of Text 102

15.1 Print Reproduction of the *panjiantu* 106

17.1 First Circular Inscription by Lü Dongbin 115

17.2 Second Circular Inscription by Lü Dongbin 117

20.1 First Circular Poem by Qian Weizhi 131

20.2 Second Circular Poem by Qian Weizhi 133

21.1 In Imitation of the Embroidered Diagram (1) 136

21.2 In Imitation of the Embroidered Diagram (2) 137

36.1 Wang Shu's Diagrammatic Poem 219

37.1 Zhang Yude's Poem set in Ancient Writing 224

37.2 Calligraphy in the Style of Ouyang Xun 226

37.3 Calligraphy in the Style of Wang Xizhi 227

37.4 Calligraphy in the Style of Ouyang Xun 228

37.5 Calligraphy in the Style of Wang Xizhi   230

37.6 Calligraphy in the Style of Pei Gongmei   231

37.7 Calligraphy in the Style of Wang Xizhi   232

37.8 Calligraphy in the Style of Pei Gongmei   233

Introduction to the Calligrams Edition

※

As if a Ring

月亮是圓的
詩也是——

The moon is round
and so is the poem—
—Zhou Mengdie (1921–2014)

It is a love story that has survived the centuries, through embellishment and expansion, rhetorical invocation, literary allusion, emotive fictionalization, and illustrative depictions in paintings. Glancing references to it appear in poems dating back to the fifth and sixth centuries. By the first half of the seventh century, the story's narrative begins to take shape with the appearance of a brief biography in a history of the Jin (265–420). As recorded in the chapter on "Exemplary Women," Su Hui 蘇惠 (style name Su Ruolan), a gifted poet native of Shiping (a town located in present-day Shaanxi), wove a brocade of a "reversible circular-picture poem" (*huiwen xuantu shi* 迴文旋圖詩) for her husband Dou Tao, the prefect of Qingzhou who had been exiled to the place of "flowing sands." This mournful poem of love's longing consisted of 840 characters and could be read "circularly, in any direction."

A gloss on the poet Jiang Yan's fifth-century "Rhapsody on Separation," also written in the early Tang dynasty, added a scandalous spin: although Dou Tao swore not to marry again, soon after his banishment to the desert wastes he married another woman. Only then did Su Hui weave her circular poem for him, as an attempt to win back his heart.

The most renowned version of the love story is attributed to Wu Zetian and officially dated 692 AD. During the Ming and Qing dynasties it circulated as a preface to Su Hui's reconstructed poem. While its authenticity cannot be proven (the compilers of an eighteenth century descriptive catalogue of the imperial collection, for one, deemed it a forgery), it's not hard to see why Su Hui would appeal to Wu Zetian or to someone pretending to be her. Well-versed in the classics and accomplished in music and poetry, Imperial Majesty Wu was the only woman in Chinese history to establish her own dynasty (the Second Zhou) and rule as Emperor. She practiced Daoist rituals and exalted Buddhism above Confucianism as an intellectual and spiritual pursuit, while supporting all three belief systems in different ways to maintain peace in the realm. A prophecy in a canonical commentary pointed to her as being an incarnation of Maitreya, reborn to rule over the island of the terrestrial world, *Jambudvīpa*. She had begun her life in the palace as a concubine; fourteen hundred years after her death, her towering memorial tablet remains blank.

In her record of Su Hui, Wu Zetian dramatized a love triangle between the poet, her husband, and his concubine, Zhao Yangtai. When Dou Tao was given a new military appointment, Su Hui, angry at her husband's infidelity, refused to accompany him and so he took Zhao Yangtai instead. Feeling remorse, Su Hui wove her *huiwen* poem and sent a servant to deliver it to him. Eventually, husband and wife reunited and their love for each other reignited with a ten-fold devotion. Wu Zetian said that the square brocade, measuring eight-by-eight inches and woven in a five-color pattern, contained more than eight hundred words that could be read horizontally, vertically, backward, forward, circularly to make over two hundred poems. To others who saw it and didn't know how to read it, Su Hui just laughed and replied, "Turning and twisting in every direction it forms poems on its own accord. No one but my beloved can be assured of comprehending it."

Wu Zetian, or her imposter, wanted to preserve the memory of Su Hui's talent in the official annals of history. She wrote that her poem "represented all of the laments of recent generations from the inner chambers and should be taken as a model by all literary scholars" and serve as a moral lesson for future generations (as Dou Tao showed remorse and a willingness to rectify his mistakes). She also mentioned a text Su Hui composed of over five thousand words that was lost during the civil unrest at end of the Sui dynasty (581–618). At some point the silk-embroidered masterpiece was also lost, along with its original design. The poem's square layout was transmitted through the ages as a post-Tang reconstruction and became known by its Wu Zetian-recorded name: *xuanjitu* 璇璣圖, or *la carte de la sphère armillaire* ("the map of the armillary sphere") as translated by Michèle Métail in her remarkable anthology of *huiwen* poems, *The Flight of Wild Geese*, originally published in France as *Le Vol des Oies Sauvages* in 2011.

Su Hui's *Xuanjitu* has also been translated as "Picture of the North Star," "Picture of the Turning Sphere," "Chart of the Constellations," "Diagram of the Armillary Sphere," "The Maze Pattern," and recently by David Hinton, who has posted his translation of one quadrant of the poem online, as "Star Gauge." "Xuan" literally means "precious jade" and "ji" means "any rotatable instrument." The two words together denote the four stars in the bowl of the Big Dipper, the single star Polaris, a prayer wheel, or a type of armillary sphere. Astrophysicist T. D. Lee thinks the *xuanji* was originally an astrometric tool made of a bamboo tube encased by a stone support called a *cong* and fitted with a three-notched, turning jade ring also called a *xuanji* (or *bi*) that could determine the position of the Celestial Pole. Consulting an astronomical almanac, he has traced it back to pre-Shang times, around 2700 BCE.

The third word, *tu*, can signify a picture, map, chart, drawing, diagram, or pattern. In Sui Hui's multi-directional pictorial pattern, text and textile converge at their etymological source in a seamless celestial weave of poetry. Art historian Eugene Wang believes Su Hui's pattern received its astral overlay during the Tang, when a historical-cultural astrological shift occurred that led to her *huiwen* poem being called a *xuanjitu*, as other visual works of the time were also named. In his article "Patterns Above and Within," published in the essay anthology *Books in Numbers*, Wang discusses various Tang and pre-Tang artifacts, like a colorful Han-dynasty brocade armband unearthed from the Lop desert in the Tarim Basin that integrates Chinese characters and animal images into a planetary design, which have an affinity with Su Hui's poem. Such artistic works he describes as providing a "visual form through which one can both reach heaven and the innermost recess of the human heart."

Remarkably, the three Tang dynasty records mentioned above—the Jin history, the gloss on Jiang Yan's rhapsody, and Wu Zetian's account—are more or less the only primary historical texts on Su Hui that all later discussions and imaginations of her life and work has been based on (besides local histories and legends that have added to the story). In the thirteenth century, for instance, Zhu Shuzhen (not the celebrated Song dynasty woman poet) is thought to have written a note on Su Hui's love poem that the seventeenth-century poet Wang Shizhen included in his *Random Talks North of the Pond*. It draws directly from Wu Zetian's narrative and goes on to describe her father's purchase of the diagram after seeing it hanging on the wall of a local official's residence, and then her own awakening to the diagram's principle asterism after many hours of study:

> The *xuanji* functions like the Heavenly Platter itself. While the longitudes and latitudes are the moving tracks of the constellations, in the middle a single "eye" is preserved that serves as the Heavenly Heart [the character xin, "heart," in the very center]. This is like the fixed star [Polaris] that does not move. The constellations revolve in their paths, never straying by a single degree, guided by this controlling star that sits in the middle.

> The Central Square [of eight characters around the central character xin] can be equated with the constellation Grand Palace. When each character is repeated once, a four-character poem emerges. One then goes on to the Second Square, which can be equated with the Purple Palace. Four-character palindromic poems are located here. The four rectangles growing out of the four sides of the Second Square form five-character palindromic poems, while in the four squares off of the corners of the Second Square one finds four-character palindromic poems. In the four rectangles growing out of the four sides of the Third Square are four-character poems, if only the last character of one line is repeated as the first character of the next line. (These lines, however, cannot be read in reverse.) In the four squares adjacent to the corners of the Third Square are three-character palindromic poems. The perimeter of the Third Square and the perimeter of the entire diagram are all seven-character palindromic poems which can be read in different directions following the boundaries.[1]

Métail includes a black-and-white gridded reproduction[2] with crisscrossing diagonals of Su Hui's brocade attributed to Zhu Shuzhen as a geometric equivalent of the spherical design which translates the armature of the armillary onto the page of the poem. This image appeared in the earliest extant anthology of *hui-wen* verse, edited by Sang Shichang and published by the Imperial Academy during the Northern Song. Unfortunately, Sang's original anthology was also lost. It was later revised and expanded in the Ming, and again in the Qing around 1662 by Zhu Xiangxian, this edition of Sang's book surviving the ages and becoming a classic of experimental Chinese literature.

A beautiful handscroll painting on silk of Su Hui in the style of Zhu Shuzhen can be seen in the collection at the Sackler Museum at Harvard University. The painting is attributed to the celebrated thirteenth century woman poet and painter, Guan Daosheng, though thought a forgery from the seventeenth century. Su Hui's portrait precedes the square reproduction of the diagram with sections of the poem dyed in five different colors and the center heart character (*xin*) absent, an empty word, followed by examples of how to read different blocks of the poem as well as Zhu's note on the brocade, as quoted in part above. Another handscroll painting at the Metropolitan Museum of Art, said to be a copy of Qiu Ying's sixteenth-century rendering of the poet, illustrates Su Hui and Dou Tao's story in a series of scenes. Zhu's note also appears with the title "Transformations of the *Xuanji* Diagram," along with many examples of her reading of the embedded poems, some correlating the constellation "enclosures" of traditional Chinese astronomy with the square walls of text in the poem.

The writer Li Ruzhen (c. 1763–1830) popularized Su Hui's brocade in his fantastical novel *Flowers in the Mirror*. He reproduced two different layouts of the armillary map: one as the simplified geometric grid with crisscrossing diagonal lines of text found in Sang's anthology, the other as the whole textual brocade with blocks of text highlighted in five colors. Li also gives detailed instructions on how to read the poem through the voice of one of his characters, Tang Min, speaking to his niece. Su Zhecong included an image of the *xuanjitu* as a frontispiece to her groundbreaking anthology of Chinese women writers *Zhonguo lidai funü zuopin xuan*《中國歷代婦女作品選》published in Shanghai in 1987. That same year Dick Higgins—poet, artist, core member of the intermedia "happenings" movement Fluxus—published his seminal anthology, two decades in the making, *Pattern Poetry: Guide to an Unknown Literature*. One can find the grid-patterned reproduction of Su Hui's poem in Higgins' book along with a caption noting it can be read in 40,000 different ways. The German sinologist Herbert Franke contributed a section on "Chinese Patterned Texts" as an appendix where he described Su Hui's "love letter" as "one of the most famous literary tours de force in Chinese civilization." Higgins' anthology opens with an epigraph by the Spanish Jesuit P. Juan Eusebio Nieremberg (1633): "El mundo es un labirinto poetico..."

Su Hui's woven labyrinth is at once the foundational text and aesthetic apex of the *huiwen* poetic tradition, a tradition often connected with the patterned poetry of *wenzi youxi* 文字遊戲 ("games of words"), though the latter was normally reserved for comic satire and light verse. The verb *hui* can be written in a few different ways and means "to return, revolve, curve, cycle." *Wen* means "writing, language, text, culture" among other secondary definitions depending on context. One of its pictographs on oracle bones look like two x's, one atop the other, and is thought to mean "pattern, design, vein," signifying the "origin of forms." Stitched together into a new word, *huiwen* has been translated as "reversible," "palindromic," "anacyclical," "circular," or "palin-textual." It refers to any text that is syntactically and semantically reversible. Unlike your usual palindrome in English where individual letters read the same forward and backward ("A man, a plan, a canal, Panama!"), *huiwen* consist of words that can be read forward and backward. The lack of articles and grammatical inflections—adjective and noun declensions, verb conjugations, agreement—along with the language's monosyllabic morphemes lend Chinese its predisposition to reversibility. So much depends on the position of words, as a rearrangement in word order can cause a transmutation between parts of speech and a change in meanings. Colloquial Chinese contains innumerable examples of reversibility. The simple sentence *wo ai mama* 我愛媽媽 ("I love mommy") for instance, functions perfectly in reverse to mean "Mommy loves me," making the declaration an infinite loop of love. And even many strictly palindromic constructions like *qu bu qu* 去不去 ("Are we / you going?") exist. But the art of reversibility is hard to master, and some types of writing are nearly impossible to adapt to the *huiwen* form, such as Buddhist chants with their many phonetically adopted Sanskrit names.

Huiwen poetry enlarges and absorbs other classical poetic styles through a diversity of patterned forms, achieving its reversible efficacy through the usual poetic determinants of sound and tonal pattern, rhythm and meaning, imagistic turns (including those of an auditory and olfactory nature), thematic continuity, visual elegance (down to the micro-level of varying radicals in a line), the elusive expression of the ineffable, and so on, thus exacting a high level of skill and creative manipulation to elevate it from a conventional game to an art of spiritual grace, infused with the *dao* 道 ("road," "route," "way") of poetry.

Wang Rong's ten-line, five-character-per-line poem "Spring Stroll" in this volume exemplifies this kind of aesthetic accomplishment. Its forward reading moves from the woman's thoughts of her beloved far out on the frontier, past twirling catkins, flowering groves, pond lotuses, the brocade curtain, and finally closes in on her aching presence in the inner chamber. In reverse her thoughts wander out in search for her beloved, from the inner chamber beyond the eastern pass north to the frontier. The two readings form an endless cycle of longing that returns and departs, zooming in and out, without ever reaching the object of her desire. The scholar Meow Hui Goh has mapped out the complex tonal prosody in Wang Rong's poem where at least three tonal patterns overlap and the shift from outside to inside and inside to outside in the middle of the poem is complemented by a diagonal mirroring of tones.

One could imagine that reversibility has been an integral part of the Chinese language since Cang Jie invented writing from observing birds making tracks in the dirt. Early palindromic intimations can be found in the binary reversals of the hexagrams in the *Book of Changes* (*Yi Jing*), repetition in the ritual hymns of the *Classic of Poetry* (*Shi Jing*), the parallel inversions in the *Book of the Way* (*Dao De Jing*), rhetorical chiasmus in the *Records of the Grand Historian*. Some trace the *huiwen* form to the anonymous eight-character "jade linked rings" (*yü lian huan*) inscribed in a circle on Han and Jin-era bronze mirrors, ink stones, and wine cups. The two "Exhortation" poems by the Daoist Lü Dongbin in this anthology are examples of these linked rings. The sixteen couplets that emerge out of each ring create an inescapable vicious loop that speaks directly to each poem's content. In the *Grand Survey of*

Chinese Reversible Poems 《中國回文詩圖大觀》 published in Shanxi in 2006, the editors Wang Qifeng et al. point to the Three Dynasties Daoist poet Cao Zhi as the first known author of this type of *huiwen*.

Liu Xie, the fifth-century author of China's first book of literary criticism *The Literary Mind and the Carving of Dragons*, had a dream at age seven of climbing into the sky to pluck colored clouds that looked like brocaded silk. It's a dream that could have been dreamt by Su Hui in her pursuit of the ideal literary form. Liu Xie said the originator of *huiwen* poetry was Dao Yuan, a mysterious figure no one can identify. He wrote, "Patterned words express the mind of the universe." The *Book of Sui* (c. 636) lists four works of *huiwen* verse dating back to the Southern and Northern dynasties (420–589), including a lost anthology compiled by the renowned landscape poet Xie Lingyun.

A precursor to Su Hui's lyrical maze that both Métail and Wang Qifeng reproduce from Sang Shichang's anthology is the illustrious "Poem on a Platter" inscribed in a series of concentric circles by the anonymous wife of Su Boyu and sent as a gift to her husband in the distant land of Shu where he had been sent on official duties. The shuttle click-clacks back and forth in the poem as the lovesick wife works the silk on the loom, heart full of sorrow, awaiting her husband's return. A notable admirer of this poem, Chairman Mao, marked the editor's comments in his edition: "This is deep love. Learn it well."

Tang poet Pi Rixiu traced the first *huiwen* poets to the early Jin, saying that the circular form, as Eugene Wang translates, "shows the tortuous wandering of the pensive mind, far-reaching and lonely. This accounts for the rise [of the art] of reversal." Indeed, it became a particularly fitting poetic form for the articulation of melancholy, giving shape to the undulating hills, the waves of the sea, the clouds of mist and fog, the "twisted innards" (*huichang*) of sorrow's figurations, circling and circling without end.

Or take the poignant pattern from nature in the title of this book that illustrates the circular movement of the reversible poem. Migrating wild geese often appear in classical Chinese poetry as a key trope (among many collective tropes) for messengers carrying letters between faraway lovers, family, or friends. They symbolize lovesickness, the loneliness and longing of exile, the sorrow of parting and separation, and the passing of the seasons as year after year the flocking waterfowl fly back and forth between their breeding and wintering grounds. Their flying formations write figures in the sky. Their route of departure and return may be the same, but the landscape beneath them changes.

Poetry anthologies have historically served many important functions, all of which center around a collective pleasure principle, as Michèle Métail's anthology amply demonstrates. Twenty years in the making, hers is the first on *huiwen* poetry to be published in the United States and continues a rich tradition of compilation and commentary in Chinese letters. About half of her book consists of a monograph on Su Hui's wondrous brocade and her interpretive reading of it, based on Daoist principles of numerological correspondences. ("Heaven, earth, and man entered into correspondences through the effect of numbers.") The other half collects reversible poems written by a range of poets after Su Hui's times through the mid-nineteenth century. These poems not only comprise visual work of mindboggling distinction but also a type of song that alternates reversible lines, as well as traditional classical poems of a fixed number of lines and characters per line arranged in antithetical couplets that follow a set tonal structure when read forward and backward. The media onto which poems originally appeared varies, too, from textiles and mirrors and such, to poems brushed onto walls and fans, or engraved onto belt ornaments and steles.

Moreover, wonder upon wonders, Métail's book comes to us translated from the French by the poet Jody Gladding. All the *huiwen* poems, too, are meticulously translated from Métail's translations of the Chinese. It is truly the "labor of many impassioned poets," as Métail herself describes the chain of transmission of the *huiwen* tradition through the ages. Some, however, might question the value of a translation move like this twice removed. At one point Métail even admits that the translator of classical Chinese poetry is "often forced to make what seems a reductive choice in French or English" and can only recreate "an impoverished paraphrase." But readers shouldn't take these modest comments at face value and should instead recall the first law of thermodynamic translation which states: Through a transfer of energy, what may seem reductive may become equally expansive and exciting in different, unexpected ways in the new language. Mary Austin's word for her translations of Amerindian poetry in her monographanthology *The American Rhythm* captures this idea: "re-expressions." This leads to the second law of thermodynamic translation which states: Each act of translating poetry is an act of interpretation that resists entropy in an open system. Here, confronted with the intricate *huiwen* patterns where the natural process of reading is reversible, Métail's interpretive dance between scholarship and art is evident at every turn through Gladding's assemblé and pirouette, interweaving the dancer and the dance.

In fact, an alternate title for *The Flight of Wild Geese* could be *Exercises in Reading*, echoing Barbara Wright's legendary translation of Raymond Queneau's *Exercises in Style*. Métail says she learned to read 3,120 poems in her reinstated color-coded map of Su Hui's brocade, and gives examples and detailed instructions, replete with diagrams on how to read them. In her 1971 anthology of women poets published in Taiwan, Yi Boyin cites a Daoist priest who found 3,752 poems in it. The reference guide *Ancient and Early Medieval Chinese Literature* notes that the scholar Li Wei read 14,005 poems in his 1996 book on the *xuanjitu*. Yin-tso Hsiung, in his preface to his own collection of Chinese reversible poetry he translated himself, *Palindrome Poems of Four Seasons* (1978), referred to a different encyclopedia that put the number of poems deciphered at 7,658. The prominent scholar and calligrapher Xie Wuliang, who called Su Hui's poem "as ancient as it is modern" in his pioneering *History of Chinese Women's Literature* 《中國婦女文學史》 published in 1916 at the dawn of the New Chinese Literature Movement, read over 3,800 poems in it. Though the New Literature turned its back on the Chinese classics and opened the floodgates to foreign literature as models of inspiration, not only did the *huiwen* poem experience a popular resurgence in newspapers and magazines (see Christopher Rea's *The Age of Irreverence*) but a new circular poetic form emerged where poems began and ended with the same words or motif to make a "pattern of return or a configuration of symmetry," as Michelle Yeh describes it in her *Modern Chinese Poetry*. But to return to the Gödelian incompleteness of Su Hui's masterpiece— Gödel who wrote that "Anything you can draw a circle around cannot explain itself without referring to something outside the circle—something you have to assume but cannot prove"—the essential matter isn't the calculation of an absolute number of readings but rather the open-ended nature of the work defined by the constellation within its four walls. Or, in the vernacular of our theoretical times, the way its ancient structuralist armature informs its own poststructuralist critique.

To see how this conjunction of mid-twentieth-century poststructuralist Paris and a poet-astronomer-weaver of the Middle Sixteen Kingdoms occurred, one must turn to the author at the center of this book. Michèle Métail, born in La Ville Lumière in 1950, has translated poetry from both German (such as the polyvocal performance poet Thomas Kling) and Chinese and for many years circulated much of her own work through "oral publication" via performances and lectures. She has called the projection of the word into space "the last stage of writing" (*le stade ultime de l'écriture*), in what sounds like a direct foil to the primacy of Jacques Derrida's written *écriture* made under the sign of music. She has created works of visual poetry, and in more recent years has published books directly engaged with classical Chinese writings, including another anthology of poetry organized around the poet Lu You's twelfth century travel diary.[3] Circling back in another connected direction, it would be hard to think of another text that altered Western poetry more profoundly than Ernest Fenellosa's "The Chinese Written Character as a Medium for Poetry"—edited by Ezra Pound and published four years after Pound's seminal *Cathay* in 1919—a text Derrida called the "first rupture in the most entrenched Western tradition," and which triggered his musings (from old French *muser*: "to waste time") on graphic over phonetic *écriture*. Fenellosa's little essay emphasized the pictographic quality of the Chinese language over the five other traditional ways of Chinese word-formation and went on to become a key manifesto for a new American poetics.[4] Métail, however, is less concerned with the isolated pictograph than in the pattern of associations prescribed by mathematical variations in reading classical Chinese.

Through Su Hui she has brought the Chinese written character as a medium for poetry into Oulipo.

Founded in Paris in 1960 by Raymond Queneau and scientist François Le Lionnais, the Workshop for Potential Literature, or Oulipo (*Ouvrir de littérature potentielle*), situated itself somewhere between the Surrealists and the secret society of mathematicians, Bourbaki, which coalesced in the mid-1930s with its sights set on set theory. In a nutshell, Fluxus, the roughly contemporaneous New York-conceived arts movement mentioned in connection with Dick Higgins above, can be described as intermedia/chance/performance with a turn toward the neo-Dada dance, and Oulipo as constraint/anti-chance/mathematics with a turn toward neo-Pythagorean texts (or possibly neo-Houdinian, as longtime member Jacques Roubaud described it: "An Oulipian author is a rat who himself builds the maze from which he sets out to escape"). Both groups were internationalist in scope and collaboratively inventive in spirit, though for Oulipo I should say "is" as the group survives to this day, with various spinoffs, while Fluxus officially or unofficially ended in 1978. Aspects of Métail's work can be seen to link indirectly with Fluxus, but it's with Oulipo she was directly involved, becoming the first woman elected to the group in 1975 and writing a number of constraint-based poetic texts as a member until she parted ways in 1998. Once you're a member of Oulipo, however, you're apparently always a member: according to Roubaud, in order to relinquish membership one must commit suicide before an officer of the court.

Oulipo's founding work is Raymond Queneau's *100,000,000,000,000 Poems*, a sequence of ten fourteen-line sonnets where any line can replace the corresponding line in any of the other sonnets. Queneau calculated that someone reading the book 24 hours a day would need 190,258,751 years to finish it. Its precursor must be the Latin Proteus poem by Su Hui's contemporary and kindred spirit, the twice prefect of Rome, Publilius Optantianus Porphyrius. In a quatrain of only five words per line, it can produce 39,016,857,600 different poems. Optantian, exiled and later recalled by Constantine the Great, also wrote a few *carmina figurata* (shaped visual poems) as well color-coded grid poems with *versus intexti* ("woven verses" i.e. secondary lines or poems inscribed in the text) that encode other poems vertically, horizontally, or diagonally, while also forming a third layer of reading as certain lines shape another set of letters within the grid. Optantian wrote: "It is a marvelous task for the mind to plait a poem in verse along various paths." Sometime in the early '70s Métail started writing her "infinite poem" *Complément de noms* ("Possessive Phrases," or "Noun Complements"), sparked in part by the music of American minimalists and Karlheinz Stockhausen. It's an ongoing poem in many sections composed of living, dead, and invented languages that "aspires to use all existing nouns without any hierarchy." Currently it numbers at least 25,776 lines. A recent installment consists of a scroll of 2,888 lines interspersed with color-coded symbols that visually denote the various markings and signs along the Danube River, which flows, naturally, for 2,888 kilometers.

"After the exhaustion of the generative power of traditional constraints," Oulipians felt, "only mathematics could offer a way out between a nostalgic obstinacy with worn-out modes of expression and an intellectually pathetic belief in 'total freedom.'" Backed by an abstract, secular science of number, quantity, and space, they could touch nature or the divine, or both, through words. They organized themselves like an open set so that one can write an Oulipian text without being connected to the group at all. Walter Abish's *Alphabetical Africa* and Inger Christensen's *Alphabet* come to mind as prominent contemporary examples. Those dead writers who wrote "paleo-Oulipian texts," wholly unaware of the group's existence, are called "anticipatory plagiarists." The list of these writers must stretch to the moon.

George Perec, author of the most well-known Oulipo novel *Life A User's Manual*, also wrote a giant palindrome, "Le Grand Palindrome," composed of 5,566 letters and some 1,000 words. Its reverse reading regroups the letters into different words and changes the punctuation so that the poem's meaning alters more dramatically than in a typical *huiwen* poem. Perec's translator and biographer David Bellos said of it: "Knowledge of the constraint disarms critical faculties; when you know that it is a monster palindrome, you tend to see nothing but its palindromic design.... Readers seem to project their own positive and negative fantasies onto Perec's palindrome, as they do onto other difficult, obscure, and unattributed works." The greatest anticipatory plagiarist of the Indo-European palindrome poem outside the Sanskrit *śleṣa* and *viloma* traditions, however, must be Russian Futurist Velimir Khlebnikov, for the sheer incantatory power and virtuosity of his 400+-line "Razin," titled after the seventeenth-century Cossack revolutionary Stepan Razin. Khlebnikov saw himself as "Razin in reverse" and his crumbling palindromic lines as "reflected rays of the future," "an incantation by the double flow of speech." But the greatest palindromic anticipatory plagiarist of all must surely be Su Hui, ensconced in her proto-*ouvrir* workshop, working needle and thread for love and the Dao.

If we create our own precursors, as Borges famously observed, then Métail created her palindromic progenitor Su Hui through writers like Perec and Khlebnikov and the Oulipian back to the *Book of Changes* and through the *huiwen* tradition, Stockhausen's serial composition by groups, and so on. It is how she assiduously decodes way after way of reading each cluster of syllabic verse, carefully tracking each changing rhyme, by combinatory means reminiscent of the Theory of Groups in theoretical physics (See Gustav Herdan's *Quantitative Linguistics*). It is how she can read a line in a hexasyllabic double-block of the armillary map 虧不盈無 衰必有衰無日不陂 (*kui bu ying wu shuai bi you shuai wu ri bu bei*) as "Everything will fade away, no moon without quarter / Everything fades away, no sun that does not set." Each chain of meaning in her charted constellation reveals itself as an ulterior articulation through active reading.

Imagine if the only thing that survived of Bach's entire oeuvre was his Art of Fugue. This gives a proportionate sense of how Su Hui's poem comes down to us—a lone, brilliant work of art that requires the reconstructive efforts of others to translate it, play it, read it, but in this case without the assistance of a body of work to shed further light on it. And like that multi-textured marvel of music, Su Hui's celestial chart is "not a form to be filled but a collection of techniques that can take many forms," as the violinist Mark Steinberg has said of Bach's fugal composition. To unlock its secrets and assume the heart and mind of the beloved it was intended for (the only one Su Hui herself confessed could comprehend it) requires an openness to read it with patience and informed creativity, a kind of "contrapuntal reading" to borrow Edward Said's phrase. Many have stared and failed before even starting. The prominent scholar of modern Chinese literature C. T. Hsia recognized the extraordinary intelligence behind Su Hui's turning sphere, but thought "the hundreds of poems embedded in the maze cannot but be turgid and dreary." Yin-tso Hsiung thought it "impossible to form good and expressive poetic sentences" from the tapestry due to "the complicated compositions and the restricted positions of the characters."

Fortunately, readers like Métail possess a different measure of reading habits, which deepened into a special mix of attention and devotion. While a few *huiwen* poetry anthologies were published in China, Taiwan, Hong Kong, and Singapore earlier in the twentieth century, for example Zhu Weigong's *Xiandai wubai jia yuantu shiji* 《現代五百家圓圖詩集》 (Palindromic Verse by Five Hundred Modern Poets, 1933) and Wang Zhonghou's *Huiwen wenxue qiguan* 《回文文學奇觀》 (Marvels of Huiwen Literature, 1976), a number of them have appeared since the 1990s, such as Wang Qifeng's *Grand Survey* noted above, Gao Tianfei's *Zhongguo dangdai huiwen shici xuanji* 《中國當代回文詩詞選集》 (Anthology of Contemporary Chinese Huiwen Poetry, 1993), Xu Yuan's *Huiwen shici wubai shou* 《回文詩詞五百首》 (500 Huiwen Poems, 1993), and Chen Linbin's *Huiwen shi ci lianji cui* 《回文詩 · 詞 · 聯集粹》 (Best Collection of Huiwen Shi, Ci, and Antithetical Couplet Poems, 2007). The Shanghai scholars Ding Shengyuan and Zhou Hanfang, authors of a 2002 book-length study on Su Hui, have set the *huiwen* poetry anthology paradigm with their comprehensive *Huiwen shi daquan* 《回文集》 (Collected Huiwen, 2012), sixty years in the making and published by the National Library of China in a six-volume deluxe slip-cased edition. If the genre had been largely overlooked or ignored for much of the last century, perceptions seem to have changed in recent years, the reversible poem even taking on nationalistic airs as a mark of cultural difference and literary uniqueness tied to poetic brilliance.

Su Hui lived during the epoch of the Six Dynasties, also known as the Period of Fragmentation. Out of the materials left from the loom, out of the fragments, we read the luminous lines of the reversible poetic form she unknowingly initiated over fifteen hundred years ago, a form that continues to renew itself through endless forms of circularity. Echoing Ezra Pound's concept of the

"luminous detail," American poet Gustaf Sobin called the Neo-
lithic stone axe-head, the Bronze age earring, the shards of Ionico-
Massalian and Etruscan pottery that he dug out of the Provençal
soil around his home "luminous debris," a term astronomers use
to describe the discs, or rings, of dust that result from collisional
cascades of planetary matter.

Another circle of thought imagines Su Hui's original *huiwen*
language to be an ancient Altaic script that predates Orkhon (Old
Turkic) by hundreds of years, possibly a mix of Pahlavi, Sogdian,
and Chinese. These are among a few of the dizzying array of lan-
guages once spoken along the trading routes known as the Silk
Road where Dou Tou was said to have been banished far from his
beloved during Fu Jian's rule of the Former Qin, first to the garri-
son at Dunhuang and then at Xiangyang, a gateway town between
the Yangzi and Yellow Rivers that had been reduced to a remote
border outpost after years of rebellion, invasion, plague, and a
devastating fire, and populated by wave after wave of immigrants.
By the time of the Khitan Empire, Hui, or Huihui, referred to the
Khwarazm people of eastern Persia, and later, by the Yuan dy-
nasty, to foreigners in general, or to people of Muslim ancestry in
particular who had traveled the trade routes and settled within the
porous borders. During the Ming, as more Hui adopted Chinese
and their mother tongue receded, the Muslim clergy responded by
setting up Arabic and Persian Quranic schools called *huiwen daxue*
("the great learning of the *hui*-language"). *Huiwen* also denoted the
Arabic-Persian script of the Turkic speaking *yerlik* (locals), the pre-
dominantly Muslim Uyghurs of today from Xinjiang, also known
as East Turkestan or Altishahr. At the turn of Su Hui's celestial
sphere in the Tang, around the time the Tibetans annexed Dun-
huang, then a vital crossroads town where two Silk Road trading

routes converged, these shamanistic, Manichaean, Nestorian, Zoro-astrian *yerlik* who later turned to Buddhism and eventually to Islam during the long rule of Moghulistan, were given the name *Huihu* 回鶻 by the imperial court—*hu* being a migratory bird of prey, most likely a falcon, syntagmatic with an eagle and white goshawk. Fragments of old Uyghur texts about these birds have been found in the caves around Dunhuang. From the hand of the Hui the *hu* soared away, circling, lines circling, jesses trailing in the wind, eye turned to emptiness, the wild *hu* whirling higher and higher then plummeting down, curved claws stretched open, closed, the hu returned, freely returning to their Hui masters with tributes of meat and fur. A half-century before Su Hui's lifetime, Prince Liu An recorded in a cosmological manual of governance for the Kingdom of Huainan: "As if a ring the spirit ends where it begins and thus attains the Dao."

Jeffrey Yang

NOTES

1. Translated by Hui-Shu Lee in *Women Writers of Traditional China*, edited by Kang-i Sun and Haun Saussy (1999).

2. Michèle Métail has reconstructed the original map of the armillary sphere (see color insert).

3. Roughly 9,220 poems of Lu You's poems are extant.

4. The May Fourth historian Chow Tse-tsung (Zhou Cezong), an avid practitioner of *huiwen* along with his friend Yang Liansheng, mentioned in a memorial for the scholar-novelist Qian Zhongshu that the latter had written an essay in English on *huiwen* poetry while studying in Europe during the 1930s. I like to imagine that this essay, now lost or buried in some archive, could have become as influential as Fenellosa's if it had found its way into James Laughlin's series of anthologies *New Directions in Poetry and Prose*, which first appeared in 1936.

Introduction

The image of wild geese is a recurring theme in Chinese poetry. In autumn, geese leave the northern regions to go south where the climate is more favorable to them. In spring, they flee the humid heat and head north. Thus they symbolize the changing seasons and the passage of time.

Wild geese are also associated with the image of separation and exile. Separation between spouses when the husband, as imperial officer, is assigned to a faraway province or, as soldier, has to join the empire's forced marches to fight barbarian invaders. Seeing the geese pass, the wife longs to send with them a message for the one she loves, and the husband dreams of following them back to his native country. Their cries blend with the plaint of a forlorn heart. They make distance and space perceptible. When a flight of geese passes, observers know that they will see it pass again through the same area in the opposite direction a few months later. The route taken in leaving is identical to the one followed in coming back. These notions of time, space, and return are fundamental to an original poetic form: reversible poems, which from the very beginning were associated with an actual story of separation. The flight of wild geese thus symbolizes both the work's structure and content.

The expression "reversible poems" *huiwenshi* (回文詩) designates texts that can be read in two directions: in addition to the usual order they can be read in reverse, beginning from the last word and progressing back upward to the first. This second reading generally creates new meanings. The reversible poem is not a fixed form in Chinese poetry. It can be adapted to existing forms or given concrete expression through original constructions that multiply the meanings of the reading. It can be limited to the permutation of the reading order of the lines or take on the aspect of circular poems that may then be read beginning from any word whatsoever. Words arranged according to horizontal or vertical lines or following diagonals or spirals can also create networks of complex signs. And finally, the characters can be organized in such a way that an image emerges from the whole, a "figured" poem.

Thus this category brings together a great variety of texts extending over a vast amount of time, almost corresponding to the history of Chinese poetry. The first examples that have come down to us date from the second century C.E., the end of the Han dynasty. The tradition has continued into our century. Nevertheless reversible poems remain almost unknown in China because they were rejected early on by the upholders of literary orthodoxy. Even today they are considered "literary diversions" and do not appear in the major anthologies, with perhaps two or three exceptions. Chinese literary critics react no differently from our own specialists who regard with suspicion any connection between poetry and investigations into form, unaware that form can sometimes be meaningful, and even reinforce meanings. The reversible poem owes its longevity and its transmission in China to a famous anecdote, repeated over the centuries by impassioned literati, that in turn prompted numerous works. Thanks to bibliographies incorporated into official dynastic histories, we can also find mention of a few collections that have since been lost. The reversible poem does not play a part in the major movements in Chinese literature, but it constitutes a singular adventure at the edge of meaning, of language and of writing. Moreover, Chinese theorists have likened it to other forms that diversify the models of classical poetry and that are based, for example, on the homophone, the double entendre, or the rebus, grouping them together under the generic label of "poems of varied forms" (*zatishi* 雜體詩). Despite surprising resemblances to a few works of Western poetry, I have preferred to retain a strictly Chinese category because, as we will see in the following pages, the reversible poem is tied from its very origin to Taoist cosmological speculations.

A Certain Predisposition in the Language

The ancient language, *wenyan* 文言, reserved for philosophical and literary writing, is characterized by extreme concision and a great capacity for evocation. The latter is due to many polysemous words and relative imprecision. A written character corresponds to a word and a syllable. As a general rule, words do not belong to a single precise grammatical category. The position in the sentence determines the function of a word, which can be an adjective, adverb, noun, or verb according to its place, and without changing "aspect," since all words are invariable. Chinese uses no conjugation, declension, gender, agreement, articles..., the only rule being that the determiner precedes the determinatum. Punctuation does not exist and line breaks follow metrical and rhythmic criteria. The juxtaposition of invariable elements thus lends itself to reading in many directions.

Some characteristics belonging to classical poetry can also be found in the reversible poem, and we must distinguish between ancient and modern styles. With the ancient style, there is greater freedom, the number of syllables per line is not fixed, nor the length of the poem, and many rhymes are allowed. With the modern style that was established under the Tang dynasty, the rules became more precise and tonal alternations—a succession of flat and oblique tones—was introduced. The couplet and not the line then constituted the basic unit. It is said to be parallel, since for each word in the first line there appears in the second a word belonging to the same category. In both the ancient and modern styles, enjambment is forbidden.

In poetry the subject is usually inferred when it is a matter of a person. Who is speaking? No word specifies if the translated verb should be conjugated in first, second, or third person, if it is a matter of singular or plural, or even if it is a matter of active or passive form. This ambiguity is not problematic in Chinese, which even promotes such polysemy. On the other hand, the translator is forced to make a choice, which very often seems reductive in French or English.

With regard to metrics, the reversible poem does not depart from tradition. Irregular lines with five or seven syllables are most frequent. In this case, a caesura is located between the second and third characters in the five-syllable line or between the fourth and fifth word in the seven-syllable line. Thanks to the irregular line length, the central character (third or fourth) changes hemistich in the reverse reading. It can sometimes even change grammatical category, being a verb in one reading direction and a noun in the other. This pivot position between the two halves of the line favors changes in meaning. Let us take the example of a parallel sentence (a text in two lines, generally placed on each side of a door or a decorative element):

風	送	香	花	紅	滿	地
feng	song	xiang	hua	hong	man	di
wind	to accompany	scent	flower	red	to fill	earth

雨	滋	春	樹	碧	連	天
yu	zi	chun	shu	bi	lian	tian
rain	to grow	spring	tree	green	to brush against	sky

The wind accompanies the scented flowers, red, they cover the
earth

The rain (makes) grow the spring trees, green, they brush
against the sky

The central characters, for "flower" and "tree" respectively,
change hemistich in the reverse reading. Beginning with the last
word, the meaning becomes:

The sky brushes against the green trees, abundant spring rain
The earth covers itself with red flowers, wind full of scent

The words "flowers" and "trees" that occupy the central position
do not change grammatical categories. They remain nouns but are
determined by different adjectives: "scented" and "spring" in one
direction, "red" and "green" in the reverse. In the second reading,
the adjectives "scented" and "spring" become nouns: "scent" and
"spring."

Thus the reversible poem requires a double translation. The
first corresponds to the usual reading direction. The second will
use other words to try to render the polysemous effect, that shift
in meaning specific to reading in reverse. As far as possible, I have
tried to retain the same number of significant units per line, but a
Chinese character is sometimes equivalent to two or three French
or English words: 冥 *ming*, for example, means literally "the inac-
cessible height of the sky," and 雁 *yan* means "wild goose." As for
doubled characters, they usually serve an onomatopoeic function.
Furthermore, the order of French or English words does not al-
ways convey the feeling of inverted terms in the reverse reading. It
is a peculiarity of the French language that it distinguishes between

a *coupe de vin* (glass of wine) and a *coupe à vin* (wine glass), for 酒樽 *jiuzun* and 樽酒 *zunjiu* in Chinese. The reader will have no lack of questions. Likewise, a character's multiple meanings are sometimes very far removed from the primary meaning. The word 團 *tuan*, for example, which means round, or ball, from which comes the idea of piling up, combining, grouping or uniting, finally comes to mean regiment!

One word more regarding vocabulary. Certain characters re-appear frequently: 深 *shen* (deep); 翠 *cui* (emerald green); 寒 *han* (cold); 屏 *ping* (screen, partition); 月 *yue* (moon); 山 *shan* (mountain). But on the other hand, Chinese has many words at its disposal to designate bamboo, according to its color, use, and form: knotty bamboo to make canes, streaked or spotted bamboo, black bamboo for ink brush handles...a diversity that our languages do not allow us to express.

The Chinese poet also has recourse to visual qualities in the writing, certain elements of which are meaningful, unlike in our alphabetic languages. A great majority of characters are formed from two parts, one being the radical that ties the word to a vague family of meanings. For example, three drops of water for the liquid element: 海 *hai* (sea); 池 *chi* (pond); 流 *liu* (to flow); 河 *he* (river); 江 *jiang* (river); and even 酒 *jiu* (wine). For the radical of tree 木 *mu*, there is 柳 *liu* (willow); 松 *song* (pine); and so on. There are 214 radicals, some of which are true pictograms. Chinese has another distinctive feature: it is written as much vertically from top to bottom as horizontally from right to left or left to right, inviting a multiplicity of readings.

All poems thus play on this very broadened perception that combines image, sound, and meaning. From this osmosis, translation reconstructs only an impoverished paraphrase of a meaning that must be definitively and sometimes arbitrarily fixed at the cost of the characters' formidable power of suggestion. Each poem presented here in Chinese is accompanied by its phonetic transcription according to Pinyin, the system currently used in the People's Republic of China. The poems are retranscribed according to the modern pronunciation of the characters. The notion of rhyme may sometimes elude the reader. It is based on the categories listed in the treatises on versification, such as "Poetic Rhymes of Ornate Writing" (*Peiwenshiyun*). Rhymes evolved over the centuries, so that in the fourth category of "zhi" words we now find words pronounced: *wei, shi, chui, qi, ju, bei,* and *yi*...

Origins of the Reversible Poem

In one of the first theoretical works on literature, *The Literary Mind and the Carving of Dragons* (*Wenxindialong*), the author Liu Xie (465–521) mentions reversible texts in the part he devotes to different poetic forms. In the ninth century, the poet Pi Rixiu (834–902) wrote a preface for one of his collections entitled *Poems of Varied Forms* (雜體詩 *zatishi*) in which he touches upon the history and development of Chinese poetry from the ancient classics until his era, the Tang dynasty. He writes:

> We find in Fu Xian (239–294) of the Jin dynasty two reversible poems with many repetitions; through permutations in the text, he increases the impression of sadness: *Melancholic, I walk far off, alone and brotherless.* That is the origin of lines with multiple repetitions. Wen Qiao (288–329) of the Jin dynasty composed a reversible text with empty words: *Mind calm, thoughts pure, to lose what one has and to venerate forgetting.* That is the origin of reversible poems.

The poems that Pi Rixiu unfortunately cites only by their first words have long been lost and it is hard to judge how they conform to the genre that interests us. However, two other examples prove that the language's capacity for reversibility was already being exploited by poets in the Han dynasty (Eastern Han, 25–220 BCE). In fact, many inscriptions appear on the backs of bronze mirrors dating from this period. Among them we find these four characters whose arrangement permits a double reading: "May you live long and have sons" or "May you always have sons (*Yi chang sheng zi/Yi zi sheng chang*).

宜

長 子

生

And then we must cite the first line of the first of the "Nineteen Ancient Poems," an anonymous work from the Han period:

行 行 重 行 行
xing xing chong xing xing
to walk to walk again to walk to walk

This line may be read equally right to left or left to right without changing the meaning, except by reinforcing its effect. The repetition of the same character four times—the single example of this in classical poetry calls up the exhausted walker who wanders endlessly, no matter the route. The central character, the only one that is different, is itself an invitation to repetition. Let us be clear that the rest of the poem has nothing to do with reversible texts and that the aim of this repetitive figure is accentuation. Yet the line's perfect symmetry demonstrates the poet's awareness of its reversibility.

Later works of literary criticism shed no more light for us on the origins of reversible texts. We cannot really go back any further than the fourth century C.E. to find a complete example, which nevertheless allows us to cover a period of almost seventeen hundred years! We will probably never know who wrote the first reversible text in China, but we have proof of the existence of many such texts. The bibliography of the *Book of the Sui*, that is, the historical annals of the dynasty that ruled from 589 to 618, lists all the works known in that period. That is where we find the titles of these collections:

Reversible poems of the five sacred mountains and the seven stars (*Wu yue qi xing huiwenshi*) in one fascicle, with no author's name.

Collection of reversible poems (*Huiwenji*) in ten fascicles by Xie Lingyun.

Reversible poems (*Huiwenji*) in eight fascicles, with no author's name.

Embroidered reversible poem (*Zhijin huiwenshi*), which probably refers to the poem by Su Hui that we will discuss, and which is the only one of four that survives.

It is interesting to note that the poet Xie Lingyun (385–443), a great figure in Chinese poetry, famous for having initiated landscape poetry, also wrote and/or compiled a collection of reversible poems. So here we have the texts that we will never read, barring sensational archeological discoveries. It is time now to move to the others, the ones that are available to us. They are presented here not according to genre but in chronological order and by author, because there are some authors who practiced writing reversible texts in various forms.

PERIOD OF THE SIX DYNASTIES
(3rd to 6th centuries)

The Poem on a Tray

Panzhongshi 盤中詩

In the fourth century, during the Jin dynasty, the government official Su Boyu who lived in Chang'an (now Xi'an) was sent on assignment to the land of Shu (now Sichuan), in the west of China. Distressed by this separation, his wife sent him a poem that she composed, inscribed on an unusual medium, a *pan*, which can be a tray, a dish, or a plate. That much we learn from the title and contents of the poem, but we know nothing about its author, not even her name. She enters posterity as the wife of Su Boyu. Her poem was reproduced in a famous anthology compiled in the sixth century, *New Songs from the Jade Terraces*, the main theme of which is women.

Poem on a Tray

High the trees of the mountain
A bird sings its sadness.
Deep the waters of the spring
The carp are fat.
Granaries empty, the sparrows
Suffer from hunger.
The wife of the official
Rarely sees her husband.
Looks out from the entrance steps

Sees a white coat. (The color of clothing worn by
    minor officials)
That must be him
It isn't him at all.
She goes inside again
Her heart is sad.
To the north, goes up into the room
To the west, climbs the stairs.
Quickly on the loom, winds the thread
Hurrying, the noise of the shuttle.
Lets out long sighs
To whom could she speak?
You have set off
And I think of you.
One day for your departure
What day for your return?
Knotting my lower belt
Promise to think of each other always.
If you forget me
Only heaven will know.
If I forget you
That fault will be punished.
My conduct is virtuous
You must know that.
What is yellow is gold
What is white is jade.
What is high is the mountain
What is low is the valley.
His name is Su

His given name is Boyu.
He is an able and intelligent man
His family lives in Chang'an, he is in Shu.
Such regret that his horse's hooves do not return
    more often!
I would prepare a thousand pounds of mutton
A hundred jars of wine for a banquet
I would fatten your horse with oats and millet.
Today if people
Are not smart enough
Give them this letter
They won't be able to read it.
You have to start in the center and turn by the
    four corners.

The transmission of this poem is a perfect example of the literary establishment's attempts to dismiss such accomplishments, wanting to see here only a poem of separation and ignoring its formal aspect. In most anthologies, it is transcribed in lines, with no reference to its directions for reading, although it ends with precise instructions. Some commentators have even claimed that the last lines may not be the author's and might have been added later. Fortunately, we have an idea of its original form thanks to Sang Shichang, author of the twelfth century anthology, *Collection of Poems Belonging to the Category of Reversible Texts*. He reproduces it as shown in Figure 1.1.

Reading begins with the central character 山 *shan* (mountain), and continues by tracing circles, alternatively from right to left and from left to right (Figure 1.2).

Figure 1.1 The original form of Poem on a Tray

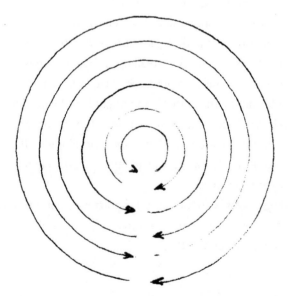

Figure 1.2 Circular reading direction for Poem on a Tray

The one hundred sixty-eight characters that make up this poem are divided up into forty-nine lines of mostly three syllables, and a few with seven syllables. Twenty-seven of them carry the rhyme. If the instructions at the end are strictly followed, it is in fact necessary to imagine a square representation in order to "begin from the center and turn by the four corners." The six concentric circles can easily be transformed into six squares and whole set of characters divided regularly over each: eight on the perimeter of the central square, sixteen on the next one, then twenty-four, thirty-two, forty, and forty-eight. Each new square increases by eight characters in relation to the preceding one and integrates the last lines, proving that they really are the author's. Here is one possible reconstruction beginning from a square:

酒 百 斛 令 君 馬 肥 麥 與 粟 今 時 人
斤 山 者 高 玉 者 白 金 者 黃 之 知 智
千 下 君 有 行 妾 念 之 出 有 日 宜 不
肉 者 誰 門 入 還 非 更 而 是 還 行 足
羊 穀 語 中 雀 常 苦 饑 吏 當 無 有 與
數 姓 當 心 倉 鳴 鳥 高 人 謂 期 妾 其
不 為 息 悲 空 悲 　 樹 婦 衣 結 治 書
歸 蘇 歎 北 肥 泉 水 山 會 白 中 當 不
蹄 字 長 上 魚 鯉 深 稀 夫 見 帶 悲 能
馬 伯 催 堂 西 入 階 出 門 望 長 君 讀
惜 玉 聲 杼 紋 機 急 忘 君 思 相 忘 當
何 作 人 才 多 智 謀 妾 天 知 之 妾 從
蜀 在 身 安 長 居 家 足 角 四 周 央 中

Figure 1.3 Reconstruction of the words in Poem on a Tray

The method of reading the circular version, alternating left and right, applies in the same way to the square version and traces the pattern of a labyrinth. A labyrinth of repeating thoughts and constant back-and-forth that echo the contents of the poem: the wife goes out on her doorstep then goes back in, she heads toward the north, then toward the west. The movements of the shuttle on the loom also resemble this coming and going. Thus there might be a correspondence between the author's straying, caused by her sadness and loneliness, and the method of reading the poem.

Su Hui: The Map of the Armillary Sphere

Xuanjitu 璿璣圖

Su Shi (née Su), wife of Dou Tao, born in Shiping, given name Hui, social name Ruolan. She excelled in the composition of poems. Tao, prefect in the period of Emperor Fujian, was exiled to Liusha. Su Shi, who was thinking of him, embroidered a reversible poem in the form of a map and gave it to him as a present. The poems obtained by reading it in circles express affliction and regret. The eight hundred forty characters result in so many poems that they cannot all be retranscribed.

That is the first mention we have of an extraordinary poem. It appears in the historical annals of the Jin dynasty (*Jinshu*) in the chapter on virtuous wives…. Yet another story of a separation and reunion sealed by a poem. This was in the second half of the fourth century. Later, in 692, the renowned empress of the Tang dynasty, Wu Zetian, wrote some "Notes on the Reversible Brocade" that provide additional details:

Su Shi was the wife of Dou Tao of Fufeng, prefect of Qianzhou at the time of Emperor Fujian of the early Qin. She was the third daughter of the sub-prefect of Chenlin, Wugong Daoshi. Her given name was Hui, her social name Ruolan. Her learning was deep and her manners elegant. Her bearing was modest and calm; she had no desire to attract attention. When Su Shi was sixteen years old, she was married into the Dou clan. Tao greatly admired her. Su Shi was anxious by nature and tended to suffer from jealousy.

Tao, social name Lianbo, grandson of the general Zizhen and second son of Lang, had distinguished manners; he had perfect knowledge of the canonical and historical texts and he was as fine a man of letters as a military man. General opinion in his time held him in high esteem. Fujian appointed him to a position of confidence. He always held important offices, and his knowledge of government was immense. Having become prefect of Qianzhou, he opposed an imperial decree and was exiled to Dunhuang to guard the border. When Emperor Fujian invaded Xianyang, which belonged to the Jin, he feared a counterattack and made good use of Tao's strategic talents; he named Tao the general of Annan for the Xianyang guard.

At first, Tao kept a concubine, Zhao Yangtai, a dancer and singer beyond compare. Tao settled her in another residence. Learning of this, Su Shi set off in search of her and when she found Yangtai, she struck and insulted her. Tao was very displeased. Yangtai could speak only of Su Shi's faults, and both flattered and denigrated her. Tao was very angry. Su Shi was twenty-one years old at the time. When Tao left to guard Xiangyang, he invited Su Shi to accompany him. Su Shi, quite indignant, refused to leave with him. So Tao took along Yangtai, assumed his duties, and sent no more news.

Mortified, Su Shi felt hatred and regret. Thus she embroidered the reversible poem. Five colors were intertwined; it was a treasure for the heart, a splendor for the eyes. This brocade measured eight inches long by eight inches wide, more than two hundred poems were inscribed there, and one may count more than eight hundred words. Read vertically and horizontally, turned in one direction and then another, all ways offered poems. The characters were flawless and the delicacy of talent surpassed any that had existed since Antiquity. It is called "Map of the Armillary Sphere." Nevertheless the reader cannot entirely grasp it. Su Shi laughed and said to people: "The poems are composed by moving about in all directions, but no one except the man I prize can understand it." She sent a servant to take it to Xianyang. Tao read the embroidered characters with great attention. He found it to be a wonder without equal, and thus sent Yangtai back to Guanzhong. With great ceremony he had a carriage prepared to fetch Su Shi and bring her to Hannan. Their mutual love was thus reinforced.

Su Shi wrote over five thousand characters of prose and poetry. During the unrest of the Sui dynasty, her writings were lost and never found again, but the embroidered reversible text was often viewed and recopied. It is a model for gynoecium complaints, and the literati regard it as often as they do their mirrors.

In the free moments that government affairs leave me, I have turned my attention to the distinguished Classics; I have often taken them from their cases. By chance I saw this map, thus I have spoken of Ruolan. I have admired Lianbo's regrets as well, so I have written these few notes to make this known to posterity.

—First day of the fifth month of the first year of the Ruyi era (692). Dynasty of the Dazhou. Empress of the Gold Wheel.

A few hundred years later, in the eleventh or twelfth century and during the Song dynasty, a woman poet, Zhu Shuzhen, found herself in possession of a copy of this poem. During a banquet while on assignment in Zhexi, her husband discovered the "Map of the Armillary Sphere" hanging on a wall. He acquired it and gave it to his wife as a present. Zhu Shuzen then wrote her own "Notes on the Map of the Armillary Sphere" (*Xuanjitu ji*), which provides some clarifications on how to read it.

And finally, in about 1200, Sang Shichang, the author of the *Collection of Reversible Texts*, was no doubt one of the last to decipher the poem in its original form. Then it disappeared like so many other works, due to invasions, wars, destruction, pillage…. No one ever again saw the square of silk embroidered by the young wife. The text was conserved, but only in black and white, neglecting entirely its distinctive arrangement.

Li Wei (born in 1932), passionate about this poetic genre, has recently immersed himself in the local records of Su Hui's birthplace and discovered valuable information that confirms what Empress Wu Zetian's text tells us. Su Hui was probably born in 359 in what is now the city of Xianyang in the Shaanxi province. *A History of the Door of the Law Monastery (Famensijishi)* reports in detail the first encounter between Su Hui and Dou Tao. It took place in 374 when Su Hui went to visit that monastery located in the west of Shaanxi. On the shore of a nearby lake she saw a handsome young man armed with a bow and arrows. He aimed at a bird that fell to the ground, then shot an arrow into the water and hit a fish. Su Hui perceived on the bank a precious sword, unsheathed, glistening in the sun and resting on a few volumes of the Classics. Since she too was beautiful and gifted, composing poems since the age of five, knowing how to paint since she was seven, having learned how to embroider at nine and to weave brocades at twelve…the two young people were immediately drawn to each other. They were married and at the age of seventeen, Su Hui followed her husband to Qinzhou, now Tianshui in Gansu. The story resembles a fairy tale; nevertheless the historical facts that follow regarding Emperor Fujian were verified. I will not give them in detail, yet they let Li Wei assigned the poem's creation to the year 381, that is to say, before the defeat of the Jin dynasty in Jinling. The house where the married couple lived in Tianshu was nicknamed by neighborhood residents, the "Terrace where the brocade is woven." An alleyway also took that name, as confirmed by a poem composed much later, during the Qing dynasty: "Song of the Alley where the brocade is woven" by Yang Rongchang. It begins with these words:

> The old alley of orioles and flowers in a Qinzhou street
> It is said to be the former residence of Su Hui.
> Among the vestiges of the past, one who seeks the workshop
> of the marvelous brocade
> Inhabitants prefer to call it the stone that bears the
> weaving loom.

Beyond the legend and historical facts, here, after many centuries, is what remains of a story of love and a square poem in five colors (Figure 2.1). This reproduction comes from an anthology published in 1992. Needless to say, no one knows how to read it!

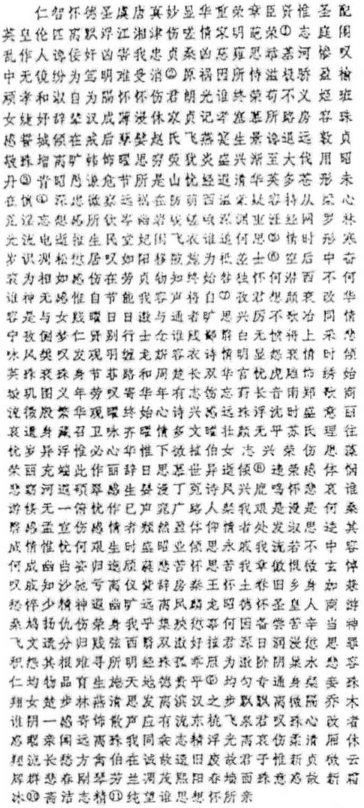

Figure 2.1 Remains of a square poem in five colors

The Cosmological Foundations of the Poem

Fortunately, the ancient documents available to us provide a rough idea of the diagram of a complex structure linked to cosmology, to which the poem's title itself refers. In fact, the armillary sphere was used in astronomy to simulate the movement of the stars, thanks to movable concentric circles. According to Chinese terminology, we can distinguish three circles there, the circle of the meridian, the circle of the horizon, and the circle of the celestial norm, to which must be added the instrument of the three coordinates of time and the instrument of the four seasonal declinations.

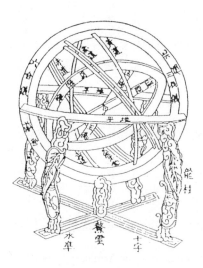

Figure 3.1 The Armillary Sphere in Chinese cosmology

The armillary sphere was invented in China by Zhang Heng (78–139). It was an instrument widely used in the time of Su Hui and beautiful examples, even though much more recent, are kept in the Beijing and Nanjing observatories. In what survives of the poem we find the equivalent of those different parts, transferred from a spherical form to a square, as this reproduction from Zhu Shuzhen shows:

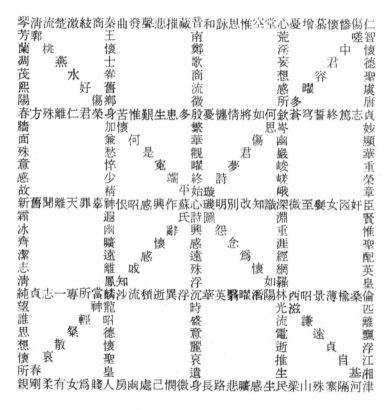

Figure 3.2 Reproduction of the Armillary Sphere by Zhu Shuzhen

The equivalent of the exterior meridian includes twenty-eight characters on each side of the poem. This is the number of the celestial houses, that is, the constellations near the equator. On the armillary sphere, they are aligned along the circle of the meridian. The central meridian is itself composed of fourteen characters on each side, and the interior meridian of four times four characters, with what the commentators call, "the map of the heart in the middle of the void" at the center. This is the central point of the poem. It is equivalent to the location of an equatorial telescope in the armillary sphere and it symbolizes the fixed point around which the celestial globe turns, in other words, the North Star. The perpendicular axes crossing at the center symbolize the instrument of the four directions or seasonal declinations, and the two diagonals the instrument of the three coordinates of time. Each part of the three-dimensional sphere thus finds its equivalent in this flat representation.

Nevertheless, revealing the structure of the poem still does not allow us to read it. The five colors mentioned by the commentators are missing. In order to understand their layout, the foundations of ancient cosmological representations must first be summarized. Early on, the Chinese became aware that although things change in appearance, the laws governing those changes are themselves unchanging. The first work handed down from early antiquity, *The Book of Changes (Yijing)* in fact demonstrates this. At the origin of the universe, two forces—two energies—born of the One enter into interaction to produce the many: *Yin* and *Yang*. *Yin*, the female principle, earth, passivity, shade, interior, inertia, flexibility. *Yang*, the male principle, heaven, activity, light, exterior, movement, rigidity. These two forces are symbolized in *The Book of Changes* by a broken line for *Yin* and an unbroken line for *Yang*:

Figure 3.3a *Yin* and *Yang* lines from *The Book of Changes*

In the first phase of interaction between these two opposites,
the paired combinations of their lines form four diagrams:

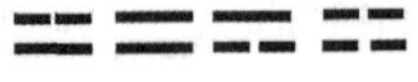

Figure 3.3b *Yin* and *Yang* combination lines
from *The Book of Changes*

Representing the gradual transition from *Yin* to *Yang* and vice
versa, these four figures have been compared to the cycle of the
seasons and the four directions: spring and east / summer and
south / autumn and west / winter and north. By adding a third line at
the bottom of each of these four figures, we obtain eight trigrams,
also arranged in correlation with the seasons and directions:

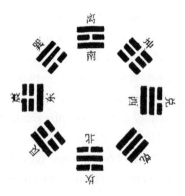

Figure 3.4 Eight trigrams

To the four principle directions are added four intermediary directions, and the seasons are divided into beginning and equinox or beginning and solstice. Each trigram also symbolizes an element or natural phenomenon. Beginning from the trigram at the top and moving toward the right:

li : south, summer solstice, fire
kun : southwest, beginning of autumn, earth
dui : west, autumn equinox, luminous vapors
      (bright clouds)
qian : northwest, beginning of winter, sky
kan : north, winter solstice, flowing water
gen : northeast, beginning of spring, mountain
zhen : east, spring equinox, thunder
xun : southeast, beginning of summer, wind

And finally, by combining these eight trigrams into pairs, a series of sixty-four hexagrams is obtained, the quintessence of all the transformations born of the interactions of *Yin* and *Yang*, and represented in two forms: as a circle or as a square (Figure 3.5).

Each hexagram has a name and refers to a particular situation according to the number of *Yin* and *Yang* lines of which it is composed, and according to its position in relation to the other hexagrams. Hence we can find: expectation, doubt, prosperity, decadence, modesty, satisfaction, halt, progress.... These symbolic figures were originally used for divination, then they gave rise to commentaries, the most famous of which remains the one attributed to Confucius.

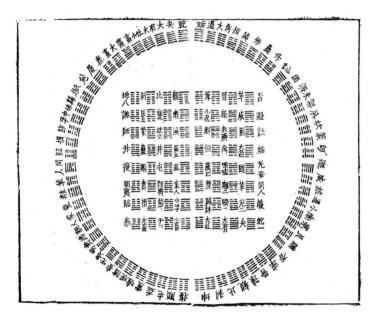

Figure 3.5 Sixty-four hexagrams

Another representation of the world—in some way comple-
mentary to this one—developed in Chinese antiquity: the theory
of the five agents. It was intended to establish relationships be-
tween the cosmos and man by means of numerology. Subsequent-
ly joined to the theory of *Yin* and *Yang*, it allowed for all existing
things to be "numbered," to be classified within a quinary, or a five-
part, system. To the four seasons was added the end of summer to
provide a fifth. It corresponded to the center (the place of observa-
tion), the fifth cardinal point. Each was then correlated to an agent,
an element.

Directions and seasons thus determined a spatial/temporal
system extending to the planets, the mountains, the hours of the
day, and by analogy, to man and all living beings. This system

numbered five types of animals, of grains, of fruits.... As for man, he possessed five viscera and five sense organs. He recognized five odors, five flavors, and five sounds, experienced five kinds of feelings, was moved by five virtues and acted by means of five functions. The art of governing, punishments, institutions, laws, military strategies, and even dynastic successions were ruled by this quinary classification. Heaven, earth, and man entered into correspondences through the effect of numbers.

A Poem in Colors

Although the poem has been handed down in black and white over the centuries, the fact that it had originally been in color has been repeatedly mentioned. Sang Shichang even points out that it conformed in this way to the five elements. Let us draw up a table of correspondences, limiting ourselves to the fundamentals:

ELEMENT	Wood	Fire	Earth	Metal	Water
DIRECTION	East	South	Center	West	North
SEASON	Spring	Summer	Late Summer	Autumn	Winter
COLOR	Green	Red	Yellow	White	Black
NUMBER	3	2	5	4	1
	8	7	10	9	6

There are two numbers per agent: an even *Yin* number and an odd *Yang* number. The first series extends from 1 to 5, the second from 6 to 10. The numbers are distributed in such a way that the second series is obtained by adding a 5 to those of the first series. The number 5 results from the union of *Yin* and *Yang* because earth, which is *Yin*, is worth 2, and heaven, which is *Yang*, is worth 3.

Sang Shichang notes in his commentary: "The poems of three, four, five, six, or seven words each follow their element and adopt its color. By seeing the color, the reader can thus infer the number of words per line." Based on these correspondences, we can assume that the lines of three syllables will thus be in green, those of four syllables in white, those of five in yellow, six in black, and seven in red. To these five basic colors, coming from the distribution of the five agents and considered to be *Yang*, are added, through transformation, five *Yin* colors. Among them is purple. Now this color is cited in the descriptions. Su Hui probably chose purple to replace white, which would hardly be visible if the piece of silk on which she was embroidering was already white or beige.

This poem fascinated a great number of the literati over the course of the centuries. Each of them wanted to distinguish himself from his predecessors by proposing a reading of new poems, never read by anyone before him. From which followed contradictory commentaries and inconsistencies in the metrical/color correspondences. By strictly conforming to the facts passed down from the last eye witnesses, it is possible to rediscover the exact distribution of the colors assigned to the eight hundred and forty (one) characters that constitute the complete text:

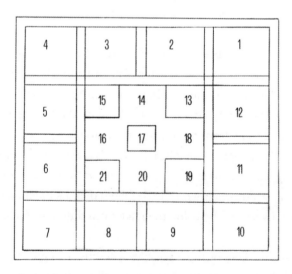

Figure 4.1 The distribution of colors in the poem

Blocks 1-4-7-10 in green
Blocks 2-3-5-6-8-9-11-12 in black
Blocks 13-15-17-19-21 in purple
Blocks 14-16-18-20 in yellow
Perimeter and horizontal axes in red

This image allows us to decipher poems, quatrains, and octets, in metrical units of three, four, five, or six syllables per line, with the even lines rhymed. Their conformity to the rules of classical poetry leaves no doubt about the accuracy of this reconstruction, except with regard to the seven-syllable poems. In fact, the ancient commentators cite heptasyllabic poems, with certain characters appearing here in green, purple, and yellow. They correspond to the axes of the armillary sphere. Thus these characters must belong to a double network of colors: green and red, purple and red, yellow and red. How could this double allegiance be rendered visible and legible in the poem? For years I searched for an answer to this question until the replica of a compass from the Han era, used in geomancy, suggested to me a possible solution.

The compass is square, like earth, but with a circle in its center, which represents heaven and on which is placed a spoon or ladle whose handle points south (Figure 4.2). The form of this indicator comes from the constellation of the Northern Dipper (our Ursa Major or Big Dipper), four stars of which constitute the bowl and the other three the handle (Figure 4.3).

Twenty-eight constellations are lined up along the perimeter of the base. The eight trigrams symbolize the eight directions. The axes representing those eight directions are formed by double lines between which characters are aligned. This pattern of vertical, horizontal, and diagonal axes corresponds to the framework for the armillary sphere. By transferring them onto the poem, it would thus be sufficient to trace in red the double lines that enclose the characters to make apparent the allegiance of some words to two categories of poems, or two different metrics. This hypothesis is in fact confirmed by the reading of new poems in lines of seven syllables with rhymes.

Figure 4.2 Replica of a Han Dynasty compass

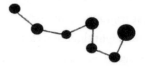

Figure 4.3 Northern Dipper or Big Dipper

We can now propose a complete reconstruction that will reveal to us the contents of this poem of multiple readings.[1] Unfortunately, the two Chinese authors who published versions of the poem, He Wenhui in 1986 and Li Wei in 1996, did not follow the color correspondences. They each propose a different color pattern and neither integrates the framework of the armillary sphere, with is nevertheless mentioned in the ancient works. The text was approached by these authors strictly from a literary perspective, without any reference to cosmology, even though its title is itself unequivocal: "Map of the Armillary Sphere (Figure 4.4)."[2]

The reader will have noticed that in the preceding pages, the commentators sometimes speak of an embroidered poem, sometimes of a woven poem. We may imagine that the poem was both woven and embroidered. Su Hui may have prepared on her loom a piece of brocade, with red threads representing the structure, and then may have embroidered the characters in color, inserting them into the spaces thus defined. We will leave it there, at the level of hypotheses, as the most important thing now is to read the poems. Let us not deprive ourselves of this pleasure any longer!

NOTES

1. Revised interpretations of this poem by Michèle Métail are based on the Chinese sources listed in the bibliography.

2. Revised reconstruction of the map by Michèle Métail is based on the *Huiwenleiju* by Sang Shichang (fl. ca. 1224) and the Chinese sources listed in the bibliography.

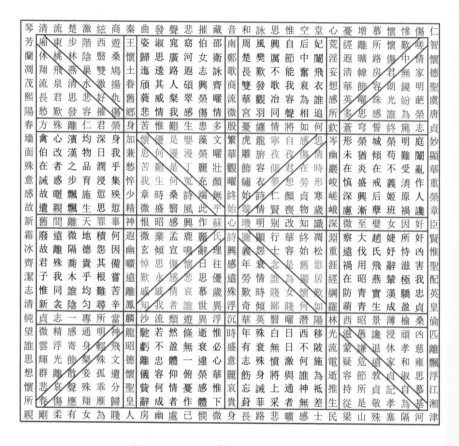

Figure 4.4 Map of the Armillary Sphere*

* See single sheet insert for a full color version, which can also be downloaded from the *Wild Geese Returning* book page at www.chineseupress.com.

Three Thousand One Hundred Twenty Poems

Empress Wu Zetian read two hundred poems on the square of silk. Kang Wanmin (Ming dynasty) reported no less than seven thousand nine hundred fifty eight, and our contemporary Li Wei counted twelve thousand eight hundred twenty. Was Su Hui herself able to calculate the exact number of poems engendered by her creation? That seems unlikely. The art of the combinatory developed very early in China, thanks to *The Book of Changes* but we are confronted here with a particularly difficult case, because of the number of parameters. The important thing is not so much the exact number of poems, nor how exhaustively we read them, as it is the vertigo that grips the reader facing the open work, facing the infinitely unfurling meaning. Three thousand one hundred twenty is the number of poems I have actually read that follow all three rules of isometry (even the number of syllables per line), rhyme, and metrical/color correspondence. Here is a survey of the readings by color.

Poems in Green

They are located at the four outer corners. Their color implies a reading in lines of three syllables conforming to the table of correspondences. For each one, twenty-four ways of reading generate eight poems of twelves lines and sixteen poems of six lines, for a total of ninety-six poems. The reader may refer to the appendix in order to find the characters of each block, their phonetic transcription, and analyses of the different ways of reading.

Upper right block, according to the first way of reading:

Alas! I sigh with languor
Over the one who wandered from the way.
Far-off the wilderness path
Wounded my innermost feelings.
The house no longer has a master
Transparent curtains in the alcove.
The face equally adorned
In the bright mirror shines forth.
Ornaments of the multiple reflections
The pearls gleam, brilliant.
So many thoughts assail me
Who is seen honored there?

Second way of reading, reverse of the one above:

To whom does the honor revert
For prompting so many thoughts?
Brilliant, the splendor of the pearls
Reflections of multiple ornaments.
Luminous the mirror shines
Elegant finery of the face.
Room with transparent curtains
You no longer have a home.
Feeling of a deep wound
The path disappears into the wilderness.

The way withdraws from here
Me languishing, I sigh, alas!

The two lines "The house no longer has a master" and "You no longer have a home" give some idea of the change in meaning introduced by the reverse reading.

According to the fifth way of reading:

Me languishing, I sigh, alas!
Over the one who wandered from the way.
The path disappears into the wilderness
Wounded my innermost feelings.
You no longer have a home
Transparent curtains in the alcove.
The elegant finery of the face
In the bright mirror shines forth.
Reflections of multiple ornaments
The pearls gleam, brilliant.
Assailed by so many thoughts
Who is seen honored there?

According to the ninth way of reading:

Alas! I sigh with langour
Wounded my innermost feelings.
The house no longer has a master
The clear mirror shines forth.
Ornaments of multiple reflections
Who is seen honored there?

According to the seventeenth way of reading:

> Alas! I sigh with langour
> The path disappears into the wilderness.
> The house no longer has a master
> Elegant finery of the face.
> Ornaments of multiple reflections
> In me so many thoughts!

According to the eighteenth way of reading:

> To whom reverts the honor
> Of the pearls that gleam, brilliant?
> Clear the mirror shines
> Transparent curtains of the alcove.
> Feeling of a deep wound
> He who wandered from the way.

According to the twenty-first way of reading:

> Me languishing, I sigh, alas!
> The path disappears into the wilderness.
> You no longer have a home
> Elegant finery of the face.
> Reflections of multiple ornaments
> In me so many thoughts!

These twenty-four ways of reading apply identically to the three other blocks of characters in the color green.

Reading of the upper left block according to the first way of reading:

Idling on the western stairway
Pacing in the eastern chamber.
Resting in the forest of peach trees
Shade covers the mulberries.
Pair of turtledoves in their nest
The swallows fly and wheel.
Gushing forth the limpid spring
The water rushes and swells.
Companion prone to sadness
I will think of you always.
A sigh of worry escapes
Face mortified by the wound.

Reading of the lower left block according to the second way of reading:

Returning, the birds wheel
Echo to my wound in spring.
Sad and afflicted sounds
Too unbearable separation.
Deserted solitary wife
Useless, abandons the world.
Brilliant with light, the ornament
Patterns bright and varied.
The light body flies
Entrusted to the floating cloud.
The discerning spirit is touched
Penetrating evidence of the principle.

Reading of the lower right block, according to the third way of reading:

> Slander spreader of ignorance
> Spitefulness infiltrating stupidity.
> Affection and pity: a kindness
> Humility and modesty: a favor.
> Fearing danger far off
> House in peace and harmony.
> Thoughts virtuous and chaste
> Honesty tempers behavior.
> Attached to what is true
> Memory of that is venerated.
> Pity is fundamental
> Respect, what follows from it.

Poems in Black

These double blocks separated by a red axis each contain eight poems of six lines of six syllables, and eight poems of twelve lines of six syllables, for a total of sixty-four poems. The direction of reading always begins from the interior moving toward the exterior.

Upper double block according to the first way of reading:

> The airs of Zhou begin with the imperial concubine
> The daughter of Wei, wide is the river, dreams of
>   returning.
> Long sighs unable to take their flight

The airs of Qi begin with "A tall woman."
For whom the elegant appearance and this enticing face?
Affected by a deep wound: my feeling, sadness!

This poem contains many allusions to the *Book of Songs* (*Shijing*), one of the six classics of the Confucian school, said to have been compiled by the master himself, which includes three hundred and five poems written between the twelfth and seventh centuries BCE. This book was the foundation of poetic culture. Moreover, the techniques of literary allusion and quotation were constantly used in ancient poetry. In the first line, "the airs of Zhou" refers to the first part of this collection, which records the folksongs of the country of Zhou. Its first poem, "The Seagulls Cry" evokes the figure of Tai Si, wife of King Wen. In the second line, "the daughter of Wei" is no doubt a reference to the fourth poem in the "Songs of Wei" in which a woman laments letting herself be deceived by "a man who seemed honest and was not." She tries to return home, but the waters of the river Qi are too high. In the fourth line, Su Hui quotes the first line of the poem, "This is a Tall Woman," which in fact belongs to the "Airs of Wei," not those of Qi. These quotes do not allow for a reverse reading, so the permutations only involve the order of the lines. Here are a few examples:

The *gong* and *yu* notes follow each other in a single music
Blaze of the sun, the sparkling green of abundant
    vegetation.
A pair (of birds) breaks into its song, I wear a ceremonial
    dress
I celebrate my ideal, the road winds away into the
    distance.

Chu Fan tried hard to pacify the women's quarters
The Prince of Shao cultivated virtue in his silent retreat.

Another historical allusion, to Chu Fan, the wife of King Zhuang of Chu.

The airs of Zhou begin with the imperial concubine
Chu Fan tried hard to pacify the women's quarters.
Long sighs powerless to take their flight
A pair (of birds) breaks into its song, I wear a ceremonial
    dress.
For whom the elegant appearance and this enticing face?
The *gong* and *yu* notes follow each other in a single music.
The Prince of Shao cultivated virtue in his silent retreat
The daughter of Wei, wide is the river, dreams of
    returning.
I celebrate my ideal, the road winds away into the distance
The airs of Qi begin with "A tall woman."
Blaze of the sun, the sparkling green of abundant
    vegetation
Affected by a deep wound, my feeling: sadness!

Example of a poem in the left two black blocks, according to the ninth way of reading:

The reason for renunciation, the warning in returning to
    Bo Qin
The reason for rejection, the eminent man dreams of
    mending his ways.
The one who suspects a close relative transforms his heart

Irrevocably gone far away the companion who shared
    my bed.
Carried by the wind I walk to the banks of the Han
Barely separated by the tall trees, who is hiding?
It engenders and makes grow the ten thousand things in
    equilibrium
Precious, the virtue of the earth in its impartial equity.
Thinking of the fault gently permeates my days throughout
Difficult to discover the root of this old rancor.
Offense and misfortune are concentrated in my being
Why must I go through so much suffering and pain?

Bo Qin, mentioned in the first line, is the founder of the country
of Lu in the period of the Zhou. He led his troops to Fei, where
he gave a famous speech, the text of which was preserved in one
of the Classics, the *Book of Documents* (*Shujing*), because he was
victorious, of course....

Lower double black block, according to the tenth way of reading:

Beauty faded, the one who composes poems
Turnips or radishes, the one who pulls them doesn't know
    the difference.
Of what benefit is it to experience only the feelings of
    sadness?
In forgetting the rules I invoke the spirits of Heaven and
    Earth.
Bowing one's head, raising one's head, elegant manners
Putting on my clothes, for whom should I behave in this
    way?

Making only one. Stricken by separation, the heart
　　withdraws
Ideals differ, aroused by indignation why expose it?
Everything will fade away, no moon without quarter
Everything fades away, no sun that does not set.
Only my death would make you come in a hurry
The years pass, the white sun moves west.

The first two lines are another allusion to the *Book of Songs*. In
the "Airs of Bei" (Book III of the first section), a long poem in six
stanzas entitled "Airs of Gu" mentions the complaint of a wife
abandoned and driven away by her husband, in favor of a younger
concubine. These words are found there:

采葑采非　　cai feng cai fei
無以下體　　wu yi xia ti

Which mean:

"Pull a turnip, pull a radish
No resentment because of one's plight (ruined)"

A metaphor for the faded beauty of a woman....

And the right double black block, according to the twelfth way of
reading:

Slandering, one sows trouble in the women's quarters
Treachery and spitefulness do harm to my faithful loyalty.
The origin of misfortune, I must accept, is difficult to grasp

What one relies upon achieves its height, pride and self-
importance.
The concubine Ban was just and did not seek honors
She refused to climb into the carriage of Emperor Cheng
of the Han.
The ramparts collapse, it is a warning, misfortune to
the descendants
Lady Zhao Feiyan was truly the cause of it.
An intense flame rose gradually like a torch
The heights achieved thanks to their brilliance are
imperishable.
Considering the depths, attention focuses on the still
unformed
Examining distances, misfortune focuses on the obscure
future.

Thanks to this longer meter, Su Hui indulges in historical allu-
sions. Madame Ban was a woman of letters who lived in the period
of the western Han. A favorite of the emperor, she was driven
away by Zhao Feiyan who later became empress. In her retreat,
she composed poems in which she lamented her pain. While she
was still a favorite, the emperor invited her to climb into the impe-
rial carriage beside him, but she refused. Only eminent men are
worthy of sitting beside the emperor; a concubine in the impe-
rial carriage is seen only in a period of decadent morals.... And
such decadence does in fact appear in the following couplet. Zhao
Feiyan is accused of causing the ramparts to collapse, a reference
to the tenth song in Book III of the "Great Odes" in the *Book of
Songs*, in which the poet deplores the harmful influence of an im-
perial concubine on the affairs of the state. It is said that the good

man builds the ramparts and that the woman knocks them down. The expression "to knock down the ramparts" in modern Chinese still refers to a woman of very great beauty who makes all heads turn. In reality, when Emperor Cheng of the Han died, his successor Emperor Ping banished Zhao Feiyan, who committed suicide. Zhao Feiyan even had the same patronymic as Zhao Yangtai, the concubine of Su Hui's own husband, an allusion hardly lost on the wife!

Poems in Yellow

Four blocks of characters in yellow arranged crosswise are read either vertically (the blocks located to the right and to the left) or horizontally (the blocks located at the top and bottom). Through their various ways of reading, they generate a total of sixty-four quatrains in lines of five syllables.

Right block according to the first way:

> The cold year is recognizable in the dead pines
> Of true things, one knows the end and the beginning.
> The depressed look deforms a beautiful face
> The virtuous sage is distinguished from the wandering
>   literati.

Second way:

> In the pine that wastes away, one recognizes the cold of
>   the year
> From the beginning to the end, one knows the truth of
>   things.

The beauty of a face is transformed by the despondency
of the look
The literati who leaves wanders far from the virtue of the
sage.

Fifth way:

The cold year is recognizable in the dead pines
From the beginning to the end, one knows the truth
of things.
The depressed look transforms a beautiful face
The literati who leaves, wanders far from the virtue of
the sage.

Ninth way:

The cold year is recognizable in the dead pines
The virtuous sage is distinguished from the wandering
literati.
The depressed look transforms a beautiful face
Of true things one knows the beginning and the end.

Thirteenth way:

Of true things one knows the beginning and the end
The depressed look transforms a beautiful face.
The virtuous sage is distinguished from the wandering
literati
The cold year is recognized in the dead pines.

Left block, ninth way:

> The *Book of Songs* begins with "The deer cry"
> If the brocade were without regrets, it would be without
>   origin.
> This intense light already declines
> The dense mulberries moved Meng Xuan.

The first line is an allusion to the first poem in the "Minor Odes," the second part of the *Book of Songs*. The poet describes a feast given by the emperor for his ministers and princes. The guests are compared to deer who are all calling out together. These are virtuous men and they bring to the emperor the teachings of wisdom. This allusion occurs frequently in Chinese poetry. The second line mirrors itself:

章微恨微元　　zhang wei hen wei yuan

brocade / without / regret / without / origin

In the usual reading direction: "If the brocade were without regrets, it would be without origin" and in its reverse reading: "If at the origin there were no regrets, there would be no brocade." The last line is also an allusion to another of the six Classics: *The Zuo Commentary to the Spring and Autumn Annals (Zuozhuan)*. The second year under Duke Xuan, Ling Zhe of the Jin fainted with hunger in a mulberry forest. Zhao Dun, the son of the duke, found and assisted him. Later, when Ling Zhe served Duke Ling of the Jin, that duke wanted to kill Zhao Dun in combat. Ling Zhe intervened and saved his life. Thus the expression "dense mulberries" is a commonly used metaphor signifying to die from hunger.

Upper block, first way of reading:

> Ornaments cover the dragon and the tiger
> Glory shines in the decorations of the banner.
> Beauty is contemplated in the made-up face
> Colors gleam in the embroidered clothing.

Lower block, sixth way of reading:

> In the decline of age, affected by the past days
> Thoughts preoccupied, feeling of sadness coming from afar.
> Sometimes I sigh, memories of another time
> It is another era, in fickleness one rarely opens one's heart.

Poems in Purple

Each of these four blocks sharing interior corners can be read ten different ways. They engender a total of forty quatrains in lines of four syllables.

Upper right block

First way of reading:

> To think of you calms me
> Sadness my feeling.
> Often I am by your side
> This dream tires my body.

Second way:

> My body is tired, I would like to dream
> When I was by your side.
> My feeling is only sadness
> I prefer to be alone to think of it.

Third way:

> I prefer to be alone to think
> Sadness my feeling.
> When I was by your side
> This dream tires my body.

Fifth way:

> I prefer to be alone to think
> To dream tires my body.
> When I was by your side
> Sadness my feeling.

Ninth way:

> Sadness my feeling
> I prefer to be alone to think of it.
> To dream tires my body
> When I am by your side.

Upper left block

First way:

> A child, I was melancholic
> How distant that seems!
> An adult, I am sad
> My life, what injustice!

Lower right block

Tenth way:

> The scorned wife sighs
> Despised and scorned, why is it this way?
> She thinks that it is an old offense
> Who lives in solitude?

Lower left block

Sixth way:

> Who knows me?
> Chagrin afflicts me.
> I sigh from eternally feeling sadness
> Anxious, my feeling is only affliction.

Poems in Red: The Armature

The axes that symbolize the different parts of the armillary sphere cross at twenty-five points. They correspond to twenty-five rhyme words. The number is significant; it is the number of stars constituting the seven constellations located in the north. The poems are all quatrains in lines of seven syllables, whose twenty-eight characters correspond to the twenty-eight constellations, the four lines to the four seasons, and the seven words per line to the visible stars of the constellation of the Northern Dipper. The whole thing together generates 2848 quatrains just by itself, probably more. The poems in red specifically offer the most readings—attested or not—and thus account for the uncertainty regarding the total number of poems because it is possible to imagine zigzag readings as well.

The twenty-five rhyme words aligned with the twenty-five intersection points are separated from one another and in all directions by six characters: to obtain lines of seven syllables with rhymes (R), two readings are possible:

$$R \; x \; x \; x \; x \; x \; x \; R$$
$$7 \; 6 \; 5 \; 4 \; 3 \; 2 \; 1$$
$$1 \; 2 \; 3 \; 4 \; 5 \; 6 \; 7$$

Thus the reverse reading is not the exact opposite of the normal reading; it is always shifted by one word. The ways of reading are distributed along the different axes and they all obey this rule. Here are a few examples from among the multitude of poems.

Beginning from the external vertical meridian on the right:

The virtuous saints who nurtured wisdom under the Yu
    and the Tang were sincere
The manifestation of honor matters to the glory of the
    government official.
Only the sage and the saint are well matched to make the
    supreme law reign
Together they wade across the Long River and the River Xiang.

The virtuous saints in question are the two mythical sovereigns: Yao and Shun. As for the last two lines, they allude to the *Analects of Confucius*, in which "The Hermits" are presented in Chapter 18: Confucius and his disciple Zilu are looking for a place to ford the river. Confucius laments that the way is not followed in the world. In the reverse reading with the shift of one character, the meaning evolves:

The river Xiang and the Long River, in flowing, leave
    behind the common laws
The saint's equal, through his eminent talent, can only be
    the wise government official.
Honor and glory reveal marvelous purity
Holy virtue, under the Tang and Yu, was nurtured by
    wisdom and humanity.

Forty different readings are possible just by starting with the character located at upper right corner. For example, by following the horizontal external meridian toward the left:

To dream sadly of what one loves increases affliction
In the empty room, I never stop thinking of it, the poem
    follows the melody.

A sound full of sadness rises in a song of Qin
On the "shang" string, the Chu air rises from the crystal-
　　clear lute.

The sound of Qin is a literary allusion that means: "to think nostalgically of one's native land." It refers to the story of Chen Zhen in the Warring States Period, sent to Chu by Prince Hui of the Qin, but he could not do without the sounds of Qin, those of his country of birth. As for the expressions "Chu air" and "Chu lute," they evoke a sad melody. The reverse reading begins with the shifting of one character:

The Chu air resounds, pure, I accompany a song of Qin in
　　the "shang" style
In the melody that rises, the sound is full of sadness.
The song is in harmony with the thoughts of a heart like
　　an empty room
Affliction increases attachment, sad wound of love for another.

Forty new readings are possible starting from that point in the upper left.

Interior meridian

Thirty ways of reading are possible, with sixty-four quatrains.

The king thinks of his land, the former life in his native
　　country
What adds to his chagrin and his dejection diminishes his
　　vitality.

In the distant wilderness the phoenix and unicorn
  withdraw
The dragon manifests virtuous thoughts, wise and
  majestic man.

The phoenix and unicorn symbolize the unusual talents of a man. As for the dragon, it signifies the talented man.

Reading of the central horizontal line:

Formerly it was said that to turn one's back on the Way of
  heaven offended the spirits
Regrets obviously arouse feelings, stimulating the heart of
  Su (Hui).
The Great Bear shines, deeply transforming knowledge
Never achieving favor, the one who relies on the flattering
  minister.

Reading from the diagonals, for example, from the upper left character and descending toward the center and then going back up toward the upper right character:

The courtyard peach trees and the waters of the Yan, my
  wounded body loves them
To think upon this unjustness begins to calm my heart.
In the poem of the Great Bear, I dream of you, sad and
  afflicted thoughts
Let the exaltation of splendor allow you to be touched by
  compassion and kindness.

Reading beginning from the center, for example, descending vertically, then from the center horizontally toward the left:

> The poem's inspiration comes from what is far away,
>> beyond the superficial and the deep
> This intention is beautiful, but affliction remains in the
>> body.
> Su (Hui) exalts her feelings to make manifest her regret
> Fault and offense are a violation of heaven, one hears talk
>> of things past and recent.

Reading combining perpendicular and diagonal lines, beginning from the upper left:

> In a distant place, your honorable person has withdrawn
>> from kindness
> Formerly it was said that to wander from the Way of
>> heaven offended the spirits.
> The affliction of spring erases beauty, gives little impor-
>> tance to the divine unicorn
> A lasting affliction becomes attached to thoughts, for the
>> time being, feelings are heavy.

Reading along the axis of the two perpendiculars, beginning from the right side to the middle:

> Wild behavior due to favor reaches what is not deep
> A lasting affliction becomes attached to thoughts, feelings
>> for the time being are heavy.

Formerly it was said that to wander from the Way of
     heaven offended the spirits
The songs of Nanzheng spreading to Shang are still not
     widespread.

The expression "songs of Zheng" in Confucian texts refers to
lascivious music that encourages carelessness. Thus it was strongly
recommended that they be banned!

The Efficacy of the Form

In this survey of the different poems contained in the "Map of the Armillary Sphere," we have yet to explore the central part. It deserves special attention because it is highly symbolic. If we consider the central block of twenty-five characters in yellow and purple, moving vertically from the upper right, we find this reading:

> The poem expresses an obvious complaint
> Beginning the Map of the Armillary Sphere is the
>   meaning of it.
> From beginning to end, the heart inspires the poem
> Nothing can calm the reason of Su Shi (Su Hui)
> It is the origin of these beautiful expressions.

Even though the number of stars making up the seven northern constellations is twenty-five, can a poem of five lines be considered? Poems in uneven numbers of lines are extremely rare in Chinese; could this be a ruse by the author, wanting to test her reader? Only a knowledge of the correspondences of color and number of syllables allows us to read the poems accurately, because there are so many of them. The sixteen characters that constitute the perimeter do not generate lines of four syllables since they are in yellow. That makes it necessary to read in lines of five syllables. Two ancient commentators explain the way of reading by reusing the corner characters. These belong to both a horizontal and a vertical line. The word that ends the line also begins the following one. Eight distinct poems appear in this way, according to whether one turns toward the right or the left:

> The feeling expressed in the poem is an obvious **complaint**
> **Complaint** whose meaning is revealed in accurate
>   **expressions.**
> The **expressions** are beautiful, they form the **beginning**
> The **beginning** of a poem without beginning or end.

And in the reverse direction:

> The poem begins, its end is without **beginnings**
> In **beginnings** I have composed beautiful **expressions.**
> **Expressions** whose meaning reveals an accurate **complaint**
> The **complaint** is obvious, it clarifies the poem on feelings.

The other ways of reading proceed by the shifting of one line, beginning from these two poems, turning sometimes to the right, sometimes to the left.

The central block of nine characters in purple poses another problem. Whatever its metrics, every poem is composed of lines having the same number of syllables. How then to apply this rule with nine characters?

to calm	to begin	Xuan
Su	heart	Ji
Shi	poem	map

Here we are in the presence of two groups of nonreversible characters: "Su Shi" (Su Hui) and "Xuan" and "Ji," naming the two stars by which one designates the armillary sphere. A reading with a line of four syllables and a line of five syllables would be conceivable:

> To calm the heart of Su Shi
> Was begun the poem on the Map of the Armillary Sphere

Nevertheless these nine characters recall one of the oldest representations: the magic square, from the *Writing of the River Luo*:

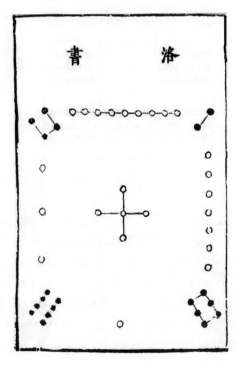

Figure 6.1 The Magic Square

The characters can be summarized in this way:

4	9	2
3	5	7
8	1	6

Each column, either horizontally or vertically, adds up to 15. The eight trigrams also find their place within the magic square diagram:

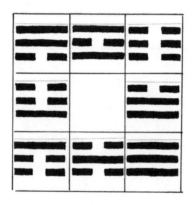

Figure 6.2 Eight trigrams within the Magic Square

Zheng Xuan (127–200 BCE) explained how the eight trigrams fit into a magic square: "The Great One circulates through the palaces of the eight trigrams. Every four translations, it penetrates the central sector, residence of the spirit of the earth. Thus, even though there are eight trigrams, they were made into nine palaces." Thanks to numerology, a whole ensemble of representations coming from very diverse sources and eras thus constitutes a coherent system.

The distribution of the eight trigrams into a magic square leaves the central square empty. The first readers of the poem indicated that there were eight hundred forty characters, some indicating eight hundred forty-one. The difference is located here, precisely in the "map of the heart at the center of the void." It is possible that the central character 心 *xin* (heart) had not been inscribed. But for readers of the time, it would have been present nonetheless, since the structure of the whole was so obvious to Su Hui's contemporaries. The order of reading for the central block thus follows:

始平蘇氏　　shi ping Su Shi
璿璣圖詩　　xuanjitu shi

Begun to calm Su Shi
The poem of the Map of the Armillary Sphere

This isometric distich rhymes and the way of reading conforms to the circulation of the Great One described by Zheng Xuan. Every four characters, there is a passage through the center. The movement created in going from one character to another symbolically forms the diagram of the "Supreme Ultimate," which represents the interaction of *Yin* and *Yang* (Figure 6.3).

The arrangement of the eight characters implies a reading from top to bottom, turning once to the left and once to the right. It corresponds to the arrangement of the eight trigrams (Figure 6.4) attributed to the mythic emperor Fuxi, called the "Sequence of Earlier Heaven."

In ancient representations, the Supreme Ultimate was placed in the center.

Figure 6.3 Interaction of the *Yin* and the *Yang*

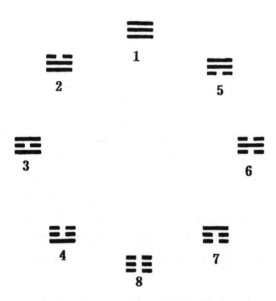

Figure 6.4 The Sequence of Earlier Heaven

This magic square at the heart of the poem is the author's signature. The numeral for *Yang* at its apogee is nine, symbol of the work's completion. The numerology is without question. If we consider the sixteen characters that surround this square, we know we can read eight poems there...the number of trigrams! Thus there is a wheeling around the central point that evokes the marvelous celestial machine. The writings of ancient cosmologists provide us with ample confirmation of our hypotheses. Ma Rong, for example, declared: "In the course of changes, the Supreme Ultimate represents the North Star." In this arrangement, the heart is the fixed point around which turns the whole ensemble of poems, comparable in their changes to the ten thousand things engendered by *Yin* and *Yang*. The nine palaces correspond to the nine heavens and nine stars of the Northern Dipper (Ursa Major). Nine stars are included, and among them the North Star (Sovereign of the Heavens), but since only seven of them are visible, depending on the case or the cosmologist's arrangement, it holds for nine or seven. The rotation of this constellation around its fixed point (the North Star) determines the seasons. In its own way, the poem's lineation illustrates the cosmology: twenty-eight, the total number of constellations, is divisible by seven as we count seven of them per season. The twenty-eight characters arranged along each of the four sides of the poem are in lines of seven syllables, constituting quatrains. Let us note further that the blocks of black and yellow each contain sixty-four poems, the number of hexagrams.

The central section repeats the pattern of the magic square and the whole ensemble that the poem forms in turn evokes that of the Palace of Light (*Mingtang*). This was a symbolic representation of the world, with a square base as the earth and a raised part, round like the heavens. The *Book of the Later Han* (*Houhanshu*) describes a Palace of Light built in the year 56. Twelve halls represented the twelve stations of the sun, that is to say, the twelve months of a year. The interior included nine halls corresponding to the nine provinces that comprised China. There the emperor celebrated rites essential for keeping the universe running smoothly. In the poem, the twelve months are distributed around the four sides of a square corresponding to the four seasons:

4	3	2	1
5			12
6			11
7	8	9	10

Figure 6.5 Twelve Months Distributed around a Square

The nine interior halls also appear in the poem thanks to the play of colors, the blocks of yellow and purple that form a cross. Moreover, these nine halls constitute a second magic square.

So, are there eight hundred forty or eight hundred forty-one characters? Originally, the word "heart" undoubtedly did not appear at the center of the poem, with the empty square as focal point of the whole ensemble of changes. It was the point of passage for the eyes that, in moving from one character to another, traced the Supreme Ultimate. Now that image, half *Yin* and half *Yang*, is in fact an arrangement with special properties, since the circumference of each half is equal to the total circumference. In other words, each half implicitly contains the whole. There exists no better definition of the reversible poem.... Each line contains its own reversal, each half—read frontwards or backwards—is equal to the whole. The idea of return, of inversion, was at the heart of Taoist philosophy and later at the heart of internal alchemy. The adept moves from the one toward the many, and then in an inverse movement, returns toward the one. In this way, he escapes disintegration and finds emptiness, and thus immortality. In the *Tao Te Ching* (*Book of the Way*), Laozi writes in the fortieth chapter:

> Return is the movement of the way
> Weakness is the usefulness of the way
> In the universe, the ten thousand things are born from
> what is
> What is born of what is not.

This return is not a closed circle but a ceaseless movement, a continual process of transformation as it is expressed in the sixty-four hexagrams of the *I Ching* (*The Book of Changes*). Among them, the twenty-fourth directly concerns the return and is composed of one unbroken *Yang* line and five broken *Yin* lines:

Figure 6.6 Twenty-fourth hexagram from the *I Ching*

The specific commentary: "Things cannot ever end, while wear and tear goes to the end of what is below, the reverse movement begins from what is above. That is why the wear and tear hexagram is followed by the return hexagram." And the twenty-third "wear and tear" hexagram stacks five broken *Yin* lines and one unbroken *Yang* line:

Figure 6.7 Twenty-third hexagram from the *I Ching*

Thus they are inversions of one another.

Two other hexagrams in Figure 6.8 present an interesting reversible structure, the forty-third and forty-fourth: "separation" and "meeting."

Figure 6.8 Forty-third and Forty-fourth hexagrams
from the *I Ching*

They are in accordance with the alternating movement of the Supreme Ultimate in which *Yang* in its full development contains a tiny part of *Yin* (the white dot in the black part) out of which the inverse process is born. Separation and meeting are the two semantic poles that justify the whole of Su Hui's poem(s).

The reversible poem truly finds its origins in China in the cosmological speculations linked to Taoism. It borrows both the spirit and the form of them. The word 圖 *tu*, "map," which appears in the poem's title, also means "diagram." It is the word used for most of the Taoist images, secret writings, diagrams to which adepts attributed magical virtues and powers of communication with the invisible world. Such efficacy is found again in the "Map of the Armillary Sphere," which is first apprehended in a non-discursive fashion. The arrangement of a network of colors, and the form that results from it, speak for themselves. They project the image of a cosmos in which space, time, heaven, and earth obey immutable laws upon which the sovereign and man in general must model their conduct. "To govern by virtue is to be like the North Star that remains in place, while all the other stars gather around it," writes Confucius in the *Analects*. The poem's form is significant. Before entering in detail into the labyrinth of the poems and their inexhaustible possibilities for reading, it evokes the changes at work in the heavens, on earth, and among men.

These cosmological references clarify for us the very concept of the poem. It may seem unbelievable that a young woman—even as a recognized poet—could have conceived such a complex system out of nothing. I favor the idea that she made use of a preexisting cosmic diagram. Such diagrams were familiar to all levels of society at that time, and the Taoist canon reproduced a great many of them, varying in complexity:

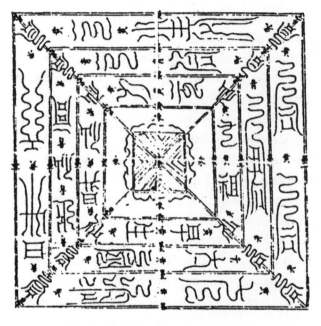

Figure 6.9 Taoist Cosmic Diagram

We can also find descriptions of elaborate rituals in which the participants moved around in the space according to axes of celestial movements. Oil lamps placed on the ground represented the constellations. Empress Wu Zetian reports the words of Su Hui who supposedly declared that only her husband could understand her poem. Maybe together they had participated in a ritual of this kind.... The ways of reading the "Map of the Armillary Sphere"—which can be translated as the "Diagram of the Armillary Sphere," let us remember—cannot help but evoke the Taoist tradition of secret writings, thanks to which officiants entered into contact with invisible powers, writings they tried to make incomprehensible to common mortals. In the most popular forms of Taoism, such as they have survived in Taiwan, one can still attend rituals and ceremonies in which these methods of representation persist, especially the theory of the five agents. Some paper offerings bear the notation: "Five agents, five colors." The cosmological substratum to which we have just alluded was widespread throughout Asia and permeated various fields of thought over the course of the centuries. Visual representations that still circulate in Buddhist circles— like mandalas—also integrate quadrangular forms with cardinal points, magic squares, with the five elements maintaining a fundamental place there. These representations of the universe are unfamiliar to us, and we cannot imagine the extent to which they were obvious to everyone who saw them.

At the beginning of this book, I quoted the sixth-century literary theorist Liu Xie who attributed the origin of the reversible poem to an alleged Daoyuan, of whom not a single trace remains. If Daoyuan is not a patronymic, those two words (*dao* and *yuan*) signify the origin of the way. The origin of the way resides in the alternation of *Yin* and *Yang*, which, through countless permutations, gives birth to the ten thousand things. The preceding analysis thus leads me to think that Liu Xie's laconic statement could be understood another way: "The reversible poem begins with the origin of the way."

From early on, Su Hui's poem was the object of literary allusions, in a work by Jiang Yan (444–505) for example, a contemporary of Liu Xie, whose poem is included in the illustrious *Choice of Literary Texts* (*Wenxuan*) compiled by Xiao Tong (501–531). Since an allusion's worth depends on readers understanding it, Su Hui's poem must have already enjoyed a certain notoriety by that time. How could Liu Xie, that great literary theoretician, have passed over it? Elsewhere in his treatise, he speaks of the "separate-assemble" (*Liheti*) form, a kind of rebus, that supposedly "issues from the oracle collections." These collections were the great occupation of Taoists and cosmologists.

Among the remaining fragments of an "Essay on Literature's Currents and their Divisions" (*Wenzhang Liubie*), another theoretician named Zhi Yu, who died in 311 and so predates Liu Xie, enlightens us on these collections. In the last sentence that survives from his treatise, he writes: "Although the category of oracle collections is not an orthodox form of literature, by taking the text in a horizontal or vertical direction, it has a meaning, by permutating it, new compositions are formed." A description that conforms in every way to that of the reversible poem! Su Hui imagined her own version of it in 381. Zhi Yu's appraisal of the non-orthodox literary form perhaps refers to the fact that it was a matter of "utilitarian" texts, written by seers, and that they did not have solely poetic aims. This qualification as non-orthodox has remained to our day, but its meaning has become pejorative. In becoming detached from its cosmological origins, the reversible poem was reduced to a simple literary game, which has distorted the assessment of it. China in the the twentieth century was hardly favorable to the expansion of Taoist ideas as old beliefs and superstitions were rigorously suppressed. Thus it would hardly occur to anyone to link the form of a poem to these speculations.

The Poem between Heaven and Earth

Heaven is round, the earth is square, but what is the form of the poem? Various cosmological representations show us how easy it is to move from the celestial circle to the terrestrial square. We have already raised this question of moving from one form to another with regard to the "Poem on a Tray" by the wife of Su Boyu. It is time to return to it in light of our discoveries. This poem is comprised of one hundred sixty-eight characters and it would need one more to fill all the spaces of a square. By leaving the central space empty, as is the case with Su Hui, the words are then organized according to a regular form. The first square at the center is composed of eight characters with one empty spot. It forms a magic square of nine elements, identical to the one that appears at the heart of Su Hui's poems. The majority of the lines have three syllables, an eminently symbolic number since it recalls the three breaths from which came the ten thousand things as well as the three constituent entities of the universe: heaven, earth, and man. The number of lines, forty-nine, corresponds to the number of yarrow stalks needed for divination when applying the methods described in the *I Ching*. The increase in the number of words from one square to the next follows an arithmetic progression by ratios of eight, the number of trigrams. Once again, it would be surprising if these numerical correspondences were simply a matter of chance. Moreover, the character "pan" that appears in the title designates not only a plate or a tray, it can also mean a pedestal or base, like that of a compass. Representations of the universe coming from Taoism are clearly not irrelevant to the creation of the first reversible poems. Even though the "Poem on a Tray" is not, strictly speaking, reversible, it was linked to that category of texts by virtue of its nonlinear arrangement. It could well be the precursor for a long tradition of works for which cosmological references offer a double reading: a non-discursive reading of a dynamic spatio-temporal arrangement that can be apprehended at first glance, and a more semantic reading, subject to comings and goings modeled on the alternations of *Yin* and *Yang*, the two fundamental principles of Chinese philosophy.

From the Poem to the Legend

The story of the reversible poem was intertwined from the beginning with Su Hui's masterpiece. Admirers of the poem often used the term "marvelous" to describe it and its author became an emblematic figure for separation. The first allusion to Su Hui that comes down to us appears in a poem by Jiang Yan (444–505), entitled simply "On Separation":

> The airs of the woven brocade, ahh, tears are exhausted
> The reversible poem, ahh, lone shadow grows sad!

Later, Empress Wu Zetian, with her "Notes on the Reversible Embroidered Poem," contributed to Su Hui's fame especially among poets of the Tang dynasty. There were many at court who were able to admire the original poem. The expressions "reversible text" and "letter on a brocade" appear frequently in poems. They refer to the story of Su Hui or serve as metaphor to evoke the letter from a wife to her exiled husband, a recurring theme in poetry.

Dou Gong in "Leaving One's Family to Follow the Army":

> Now it is thus, the wife whose husband left for a long
> voyage
> Loves to embroider a reversible poem and send it to Dou
> Tao.

Li Bo in "Addressing a Mailing Lost Distance":

> Weaving a brocade in the guise of a short letter
> Feelings conform to combinations in the reversible poem.

Li Qiao in "Ballad of the Solitary Woman":

> On the round fan, the words testify to love
> The reversible poem was sent to the one who suffers.

Wen Tingyun in "Sent to the Secretary Guo of Bingzhou":

> The cavalry patrol sends no message
> It is useless to put the reversible poem on the loom.

This allusion means that Secretary Guo has not left on an expedition.

Li Pin in "Ancient Thoughts":

> Even though one is not the wife of Dou Tao
> The characters embroidered on the brocade already form
>   a poem.

Li Bo in another poem, "Long Separated":

> A letter on brocade arrived
> When he unseals it, the man sighs sadly.

Zheng Xi in "Thoughts of a Thousand Li" signifies the absence of news:

> In autumn, the sea stops conveying the letter in silk
> At night, the loom no longer weaves the brocade.

Dou Gong in another poem, "Song of the Young Wife":

> The dream whirls beyond the peaks of Heaven (*Tianshan*)
> Melancholy is read in the brocade.

In the Tang dynasty alone, more than thirty poems mention the work of Su Hui, not counting the authors who refer to it by adopting the reversible form, as we will see in the following pages.

The great Song poet Huang Tingjian (1045–1105) wrote a quatrain on Su Hui:

> A thousand embroidered poems compose the reversible
>   poem brocade
> How could Yangtai equal it in the evening rain?
> There is also the skillful hand of Su Hui
> Only Dou Lianpo did not have regrets.

Since the Chinese were great archivists and compilers of catalogues of works, we also know that many short stories were devoted to the history of Su Hui during the Tang dynasty, although unfortunately not a single one survives. In 1798, more than a century after his death, a novel appeared that was attributed to the famous Li Yu (1611–1679), the author of the very erotic *The Flesh as Prayer Rug*. In the *Story of the Reversible Text on a Reconstructed*

Brocade (Hejing Huiwenzhuan), he was quite heavily inspired by the anecdote of Su Hui. Honest or corrupt government officials, devoted or ingrate sons, valiant warriors and highwaymen, are found brushing elbows in this story with its many sudden twists that sometimes call upon the fantastic or the supernatural. The author locates the action in the time of the Tang dynasty and he begins by recalling the story of Su Hui. Then the scholar Liang appears, on the road back home from the capital where he has just passed the officials exams. By chance, he finds half of the brocade embroidered by Su Hui. He acquires it, and his wife Doushi recognizes it as soon as she sees it because the brocade once belonged to her family. This couple gives birth to Liang Sheng, a child gifted with extraordinary talents. He knows how to write at the age of seven. When he sees the "Map of the Armillary Sphere," he amuses himself by deciphering new poems there. Word of this prodigy spreads and Liang Sheng is invited to go to the prefect of the region, Liu. The boy begins his studies to become a government official. All the rich families of the town of Xiangzhou who have marriageable daughters dream of having him as their son-in-law. However, Liang Sheng feels such deep admiration for this poem that he will only consent to marry a young woman gifted with the same talents as Su Hui. There are many candidates, but none of them touches his heart!

A new prefect is named in Xiangzhou: Sang, who dies before taking up his position. He leaves an orphan, Menglan, whose birth was marked by extraordinary events. While her mother was pregnant, an apsara appeared to her in a dream. In one hand the goddess held an orchid, in the other, half a brocade embroidered in five colors. On the night of Menglan's first birthday—the girl's name means orchid, as in the dream—a light rose from the earth. A coffer appeared containing the half brocade. The girl's father shows it to her for the first time when she is seven years old. Her mind is so quick that she is immediately able to decipher the poems. In accordance with the apsara's instructions, she would only consent to marry the one who possessed the other half of the brocade.

The novel's plot consists of reuniting the two halves of the poem and thus the two young people. Liang Sheng and Menglan are engaged and exchange their two halves of the brocade as a pledge of fidelity. A series of events separates them from one another. After the two heroes have escaped death and numerous traps, the two halves of the poem are finally rejoined.

Menglan has a cousin, the beautiful and intelligent Menghui, who shares her passion for the reversible text. Menglan thus schemes so that her husband will also choose Menghui as a wife. Menglan as Su Hui, Menghui as Zhao Yangtai, and Liang Sheng as Dou Tao: here we have a ménage à trois that exists in perfect harmony thanks to the reversible poem. The brocade is rejoined, and a conjugal union is assured! The descendants of the three heroes inherit the "Map of the Armillary Sphere" until one day there is the sound of celestial music and the brocade disappears in the midst of colored clouds and scented winds.

In the last chapter of the novel, Liang Sheng finds himself in the presence of the emperor, to whom he presents twenty-eight quatrains of reversible lines, variations on a poem composed by his two wives:

天上飛仙飛下天	tian shang fei xian fei xia tian
世人留得錦來傳	shi ren liu de jin lai chuan
篇分字讀章分句	pian fen zi du zhang fen ju
千萬詩成愁萬千	qian wan shi cheng chou wan qian

From the heavens an immortal descends to earth
Men of this world conserve the brocade to pass it on.

The lines read word by word, the stanzas read line by line
Form thousands of poems of infinite sadness.

The distinctive feature of the reverse reading is that the immortal reascends to heaven! In the first line, "tian shang" means "in the heavens," and "tian xia" means "under the heavens," that is to say, on earth. Inversely, "shang tian" means "to ascend to heaven" and "xia tian" to descend from heaven. Thus the second reading goes like this:

An infinite sadness engenders thousands of poems
With lines read by stanzas, with words read by lines.
The brocade passed on is conserved among men
The immortal descended to earth reascends to the heavens.

Liang Sheng offers many variations in this heptasyllabic quatrain. The emperor is filled with wonder at what it is possible to make with the twenty-eight characters:

The son of heaven looked at it and said with a sigh, "I never thought that so many lines could be hiding in twenty-eight characters. Whether you read them vertically or horizontally, in the right direction or backwards, whether you add or subtract characters, whether you lengthen or shorten the line, not one reading doesn't offer a meaning. This is a new 'Map of the Armillary Sphere by Su Shi!'"

A second author, Li Ruzhen (1763–1830) showed an interest in Su Hui in the novel he wrote in 1828, *The Fate of the Flowers in the Mirror (Jing huayuan)*. He devotes the forty-first chapter to her, providing valuable information on the ways of reading the poem.

The painters were not to be outdone; many staked their claim on the anecdote, making it a subject for their own artwork. First in the Tang dynasty, with two great masters: Zhang Xuan (714–742), who specialized in painting aristocratic women and beauties of the gynoecium, and his contemporary Zhou Fang, who also preferred courtly subjects. In 1802, Li Gonglin saw and described a series of six paintings dating from the Tang, without specifying who painted them. Three represented Su Hui at home weaving the brocade and three involved Dou Tao's invitation to rejoin him, the carriage sent for Su Hui, and her welcome, with young women seated on carpets playing music. The empress' preface was calligraphed there as well, and the poem reproduced. Li Gonglin notes that the colors in these paintings were already faded. Under the Ming, Qiu Ying (sixteenth century), a specialist in portraits, also produced three scrolls tracing this story (Figure 8.1). They are held in the Metropolitan Museum of Art in New York. The same scenes are represented there: the creation of the poem and its delivery, the carriage sent by Dou Tao, and Su Hui's reception, to which are added a portrait of the young woman, the poem reproduced in many plates, and Wu Zetian's preface.

In 1771, Kong Guanglin noted the existence of a painting almost identical to the description by Li Gonglin. In the preface to his play, "The Brocade of the Armillary Sphere" (*Xuanji jin*), he writes that someone possessed a scroll dating from the Yuan (1277–1367), the theme of which was this poem. His father wanted to buy it but the seller was asking too high a price. What appeared there was, first, a reproduction of the poem, second, information on the ways of reading it, and finally, four scenes representing the weaving, the sending, the reading by Dou Tao, and finally the reunion of the two spouses. According to the author, this painting was supposedly made by following an account from the Tang period.

Figure 8.1 *Lady Su Hui and Her Verse Puzzle*[1]

One day when Kong Guanglin was sick and confined to his bed, the thought of this scroll returned to him. He was inspired to write a play in four acts: "The Brocade of the Armillary Sphere." This took the form of "Zaju," a traditional Chinese drama with alternating sung and spoken passages. Various types of characters appear there: the principal female role (Su Hui), secondary female roles (old woman, servant), principal male role (Dou Tao) and so on. First we see Su Hui lamenting, then embroidering her poem. A servant is then sent to deliver it to Dou Tao. The third act describes in detail the ways of reading it. The last act is obviously devoted to the couple's reunion, as happy as their courtship.

Figure 8.2 The Principle Female Role (Su Hui)

The British Museum holds a collection of books and paintings related to Su Hui, including one portrait, the whole of which belonged to Guan Daosheng. Let us also take note of the many wood engravings—illustrations of the works of Li Yu and Li Ruzhen, and the "Album of One Hundred Beauties" (*Baimei tupu*) in which the images later codified in this story are tirelessly reproduced.

Parallel to her celebrity status in literary circles, Su Hui became a legendary figure in the region of her birth, Shaanxi. This story takes a more tragic turn, no doubt imbued with the hardships endured by those who lived there. Upon receiving his wife's poem, Dou Tao fled his exile in Dunhuang in order to rejoin her. When he arrived, she had hung herself and her body had disappeared. According to the legend, the emperor, who lived a life of debauchery, knew of Su Hui's poem and admired it. So he sent a eunuch bearing a decree announcing that Dou Tao had died in the imperial marches and that he was inviting Su Hui to join him at his palace because he wanted to make her his concubine. Indignant, Su Hui cut off her beautiful hair and committed suicide to escape that dishonor. Inconsolable, Dou Tao supposedly had her poem engraved on a black stone slab and mounted on the wall screening the north entrance of their home in the village of Gumeiyang.

Since this story has been endlessly embroidered, another version holds that the prefect Dou Tao had disobeyed an order from the emperor and was exiled in the wilderness and all his possessions were confiscated. Su Hui remained with her mother and daughter. Their life became increasingly difficult. So the young wife wove handkerchiefs in threads of many colors with reversible poems on them. Underneath she embroidered the words, "The sparrows of the field enliven the spring, a pair of cranes open their wings," imploring the emperor for clemency. For years she sold them on the streets to survive. One handkerchief reached the court, at Chang'an. The story moved the ministers, and the emperor finally got word of it. Amazed by the exceptional talents of this young woman, he immediately had Dou Tao called back. Dou Tao rejoined his wife and the couple lived happily ever after. The text inscribed on those handkerchiefs has come down to us. The one hundred and twelve characters that it includes in fact generate only one reading. The "reversibility" inheres in the gestures that must be performed in order to read it, because the characters are inscribed in all directions, diagonally, backwards...which again recalls the methods of secret writing widely used in Taoist circles.

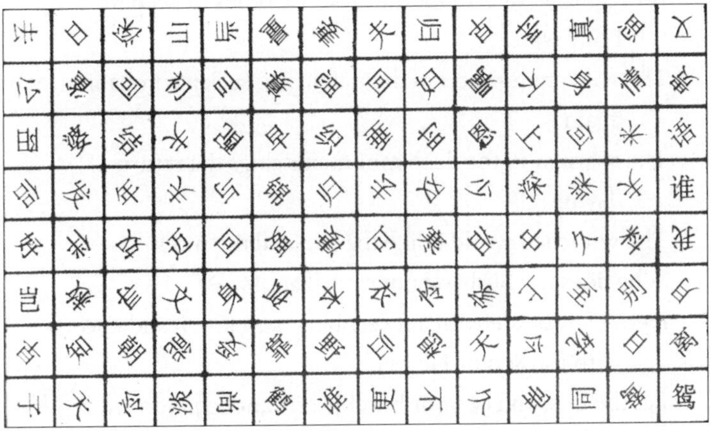

Figure 8.3 Reversible poems in an embroidered handkerchief[2]

Reading begins with the character located at the top in the seventh square starting from the right, and ends in the eighth square beside it after having progressed square by square. The result is a poem in sixteen lines with seven syllables each:

Between the spouses a deep affection, they have long been
    separated
On the pillows of the nuptial bed, tears fall in pairs.
Reflecting on the moment of being newlywed
Who would have guessed the indifference the lonely wife
    would suffer?
In days gone by words of true feeling were confided
Who would think they would have fallen silent for so
    long now?
In fact I would like to leave the same day as my husband
My parents-in-law grow old, upon whom will they rely?
I think too that at home firewood and rice are expensive
And think as well about the lack of clothes to keep the
    body warm.
The wild cranes excel in their ability to seek a companion
    again
The sparrow in the deep mountains sings the return of
    dawn.
The wretched world is like the sun and the moon
Why does my husband not return at dawn?
I wove a brocade with a reversible poem for an audience
    with the Son of Heaven
Let the husband of your humble servant be pardoned
    early so he can rejoin his wedded wife.

Su Hui's poem comes down to us thanks to the story that
determined its creation and may almost overshadow it. It neverthe-
less prompted very lively creative competition, especially among
women, who tried to outdo one another in ingenuity to invent ex-
traordinary new texts. As early as the Jin dynasty, Li Ying, a woman,

composed a poem of one thousand five hundred twenty-one char-
acters on the model of the "Map of the Armillary Sphere." It is said
to have engendered many thousands of poems. Even though this
poem is lost, an ample number of others like it still survive.

NOTES

1. *Lady Su Hui and Her Verse Puzzle*, 16th century, Ming Dynasty (1368–1644), in
the style of Qiu Ying (Chinese, ca. 1495–1552). Handscroll; ink and color on silk,
10 ¹⁄₁₆ in. x 10 ft. 2 ¾ in. The Metropolitan Museum of Art, www.metmuseum.org.

2. Original diagram from *Shaanxi Difangchi*. Current reproduction from Li Wei,
Shiyuan zhenpin, Xuanjitu, Dongfang chubanshe, 1996, p. 17.

He Daoqing (5th century)

We know nothing about this poet. His text only shows us that he knew the story of Su Hui.

四言	si yan
陽春艷曲	yang chun yan qu
麗錦誇文	li jin kua wen
傷情織怨	shang qing zhi yuan
長路懷君	chang lu huai jun
惜別同心	xi bie tong xin
膺填思悄	ying tian si qiao
碧鳳香殘	bi feng xiang can
金屏露曉	jin ping lu xiao
入夢迢迢	ru meng tiao tiao
抽詞軋軋	chou ci ya ya
泣寄回波	qi ji hui bo
詩緘去札	shi jian qu zha

Poem in Lines of Four Syllables

In spring, an elegant air
On a pretty brocade, a vast text.
Feelings of affliction weave the plaint
A long path, languishing for the master.
Regretfully separated from a similar heart

The inner depths fill with sad thoughts.
Green phoenix in the fading scents
Gilded screen in the dawn moist with dew.
Beginning to dream, faraway, faraway
Making the words arise, toc, toc (noise of
    the shuttle on the loom)
Confided in tears to the swirling waves
The poem is sealed, the letter sent.

*

The letter is sent, the poem sealed
The swirling waves convey tears.
Toc, toc, the words arise
Faraway, faraway, one enters there in dream.
Dew of the dawn, gilded screen
Fading scents, green phoenix.
Sad thoughts are filling the inner depths
Hearts resemble each other, separation is regret.
The master laments that the path is long
In the complaint wounded feelings are woven.
The text is vast, the brocade pretty
The song is beautiful, the spring sunny.

Wang Rong (468–494)

Wang Rong's fate was not enviable, and unfortunately not uncommon in the circles of the Chinese literati close to power. He spent his last days in prison where he was granted the special favor of being able to commit suicide. Among his few remaining poems, three are reversible.

春遊	chun you
枝分柳塞北	zhi fen liu sai bei
葉暗榆關東	ye an yu guan dong
垂條逐絮轉	chui tiao zhu xu zhuan
落蕊散花叢	luo rui san hua cong
池蓮照曉月	chi lian zhao xiao yue
幔錦拂朝風	man jin fu zhao feng
低吹雜綸羽	di chui za guan yu
薄粉艷妝紅	bo fen yan zhuang hong
離情隔遠道	li qing ge yuan dao
難結深閨中	nan jie shen gui zhong

Spring Stroll

Branching boughs of willows north of the frontier
Dark leaves of elms east of the pass.
In hanging branches twirl catkins
Falling buds scatter in flowering groves.
Pond lotuses are lit by the brilliant moon

Brocaded curtain stirs in morning wind.
Tossed to the ground pell-mell, cap and fan
A fine powder, distinguished red of make-up.
Feelings of separation and obstacles in a distant road
How difficult they are to dispel in the depths of the
women's quarters.

*

In the women's quarters at the heart, deep ties are difficult
to bear
The road grows distant, feelings of separation are
forgotten.
Made up with rouge, the distinguished powder is fine
Fan and cap are tossed pell-mell to the ground.
Wind of early morning stirs the damasked curtain
The moon shines, lights the pond of lotuses.
Flowers in groves scatter their buds that fall
Twirling catkins pursue branches that hang.
At the eastern pass, elms in dark flower
At the northern frontier, willows with branching boughs.

後園作回文詩   huo yuan zuo hui wen shi

斜蜂繞徑曲	xie feng rao jing qu
聳石帶山連	song shi dai shan lian
花餘拂戲鳥	hua yu fu xi niao
樹密陰鳴蟬	shu mi yin ming chan

Reversible Poem Composed in the Imperial Garden

Sloping peaks divert the winding path
Erected stones form a mountainous chain.

Abundant flowers brush against birds at play
Dense trees shelter cicadas that sing.

*

Cicadas sing and hide in thick trees
Birds play and stir abundant flowers.
Mountains touch, amassing height of stones
The winding path coils up the slopes of peaks.

In contemplating this landscape, we move from the distant to the close and from the close to the distant.

Wang Rong's other poem belongs to a special category of reversible texts: *fan fu* 反覆 (turn and return). The words are arranged in a circle, and the reader can begin with any character and read in one direction or the other. With twenty words, Wang Rong composed forty pentasyllabic quatrains with intersecting rhymes.

Figure 10.1 Wang Rong's Reversible Text

Motionless fog near green trees
Last snow on the pavilion where sun breaks through.
Icy sky penetrates the watchtower on the summit
The cold moon accompanies the boat that moves off.

Penetrating sky, cold pavilion where sun breaks through
Withstanding snow, bent trees are green.
In fog a boat, peaceful, moves off
Bearing the moon, icy summit of the watchtower.

Pavillion where sun breaks through, icy sky is penetrating
Watchtower of the summit, cold moon leads there.
A boat grows distant, motionless fog is near
Green trees, the last snow hides there.

...and so on

This form lends itself to the description of landscapes. The poet plays with distance, near and far, with points of view and lighting. From one reading to the next, the variations are minuscule, but they contribute to an impressive vision of the landscape, a veritable poetic kaleidoscope.

Yin Zhongkan (5th century)

There were also more decorative circular inscriptions engraved on the backs of mirrors, wine trays, and ink stones, or calligraphed on round fans. Usually with eight characters, they made up sequences of sixteen couplets. These were more a matter of maxims, of little literary significance except that they confirmed the early Chinese interest in reversible texts and combinative words. This inscription by Yin Zhongkan appeared on a wine tray:

Figure 11.1 Reversible Inscription by Yin Zhongkan

Among the sixteen possible readings:

> The rule is to have what suits the body
> Joy and wine which becomes ritual.

> Wine is the ritual rule
> Having what suits, the body is joyous.

What delights the body, it is suitable to have it
What rules the rituals, it is wine.

What suits the body is joy and wine
For rituals, there are rules.

The Xiao Court

In the sixth century, Xiao Yan (502–549), Emperor Wu of the Liang dynasty, surrounded himself with a brilliant court frequented by the greatest authors of the period. These aristocrats loved to gather, often in a beautiful garden, where they drank, did calligraphy, and improvised poems. Xiao Yan also composed an inscription for an ink stone, with sixteen ways to read it:

Figure 12.1 Reversible Inscription by Xiao Yan

Writing virtuously shapes the words
Using ink to paint the heart...and so on.

Xiao Gang (503–551), Emperor Jian Wen of the same dynasty, calligraphed an inscription on a round fan:

Figure 12.2 Reversible Inscription by Xiao Gang

The moon in the emptiness lights the hoar frost
Snow in the wind makes the light sparkle...and so on.

The title of a sequence of reversible quatrains composed in the imperial garden gives us an idea of these brilliant gatherings. These were poems composed in response to Xiao Yi (508–555), the emperor's younger brother. More than a hundred of his poems survive. The subject and rhyme scheme were imposed as part of the standard rules for these poetic games. Yu Xin (513–581), the most famous poet of the period, was also present that day:

早連生竭蠖	zao lian sheng jie huo
嫩菊養秋粼	nen ju yang qiu lin
滿地留浴鷺	man di liu yu lu
分橋上戲人	fen qiao shang xi ren

Early lotuses grow, emptying the pool
Delicate chrysanthemums feed on the clear waters of
    autumn.
Covering the ground, egrets settle after bathing
Climbing the split bridge, people at play.

*

People at play, they climb to the middle of the bridge
Egrets bathe, (then) take over the whole ground.
The clear waters of autumn delicately feed the
    chrysanthemums
The pool empties, making the lotuses grow early.

By Xiao Gang:

忮雲間石蜂　　zhi yun jian shi feng
脈水浸山岸　　mai shui jin shan an
池清戲鵠聚　　chi qing xi hu ju
樹秋飛葉散　　shu qiu fei ye san

Between dispersed clouds, rocky peaks
Waters flow, filter through mountainous slopes.
On the clear pond a flock of swans play
From the autumn trees, twirling leaves scatter.

*

Scattered leaves fly, autumn trees
Gathered swans play, clear pond.
In the high mountains penetrate veins of water
The rocks of the summits divide strands of clouds.

By Xiao Lun (507–551), brother of Xiao Gang:

燭花臨靜夜　　zhu hua lin jing ye
香氣入重幃　　xiang qi ru zhong wei
曲度聞歌遠　　qu du wen ge yuan
繁弦覺舞遲　　fan xian jue wu chi

The candle stub keeps watch over the calm night
The scented air penetrates the heavy curtains.
The piece composed, hearing the song that grows fainter
The many strings (of the instrument) signal that the dance
　　is slowing down.

*

The slow dance reveals the multiplicity of strings
    (of the instrument)
The distant song is heard in the composition.
The curtains again penetrate the scents of the air
The calm night descends on the colored candles. (colored
    candles are reserved for weddings)

By Xiao Zhi, during that same gathering:

危台出岫烱	wei tai chu xiu jiong
曲間上橋斜	qu jian shang qiao xie
池連隱弱芰	chi lian yin ruo ji
徑筱落藤花	jing xiao luo teng hua

The high terrace overlooks distant peaks
Over the winding falls, a lopsided bridge.
The pond lotuses conceal fragile water chestnuts
Dwarf bamboo along the path collect the blossoms of the
    climbing plants.

*

Creepers in blossom fall onto the path of dwarf bamboo
Water chestnuts delicately cover the lotus pond.
The diagonal bridge spans a winding waterfall
Distant peaks rise above steep terraced slopes.

Independently of this sequence, Xiao Zhi composed another
reversible poem:

六言   liu yan

青山映雪含思	qing shan ying xue han si
碧草抽煙系情	bi cao chou yan xi qing
屏香夢愁月落	ping xiang meng chou yue luo
桌蘭吟苦風清	zhuo lan yin ku feng qing
零珠淚紅珍促	ling zhu lei hong zhen cu
摻雲娥翠杯停	can yun e cui bei ting
聽君唱我離恨	ting jun chang wo li hen
聲悲心淒骨驚	sheng bei xin qi gu jing

Poem in Lines of Six Syllables

The green mountain is reflected in the snow, thoughts
    contained
The bluish grass emerges from the mist, feelings of
    attachment.
Scent of the folding screen, the dream is sad, the moon
    sets
Orchids on the table, the song is sorrowful, the wind
    freshens.
Drops form, tears of blood overwhelm
Dark clouds over painted brows, the cup stops.
When I hear you sing, my resentment fades away
The sound is captivating, the heart plaintive, the body
    shaken.

In some Chinese gardens, visitors can still see small, very sinu-
ous artificial canals through which water circulates. During poetic
gatherings, participants sat on their banks. Cups of wine were

regularly put in the water where they floated along, carried by the current. When a cup stopped before a participant, he was obliged to improvise a poem on the spot. The most famous of these gatherings was held in the spring of 353 at the Pavilion of Orchids, at the initiative of the great calligrapher Wang Xizhi. That is the meaning of "the cup stops" in this poem.

In reverse:

> The body restless, the heart desolate, the voice is plaintive
> Hating the separation, I sing, you hear me.
> Beauty stops the cup, dark clouds
> Overwhelmed with suffering, tears of blood flow.
> Light wind, singing with sorrow, the table of orchids
> Setting moon, dreaming sadly of the scented folding
> > screen.
> Feelings attached to the fog that lifts, emerald green grass
> Thoughts retain reflections of the snow, green mountain.

During the four centuries covered by the period known as the Six Dynasties, many other reversible poems were no doubt written. Some may still be hiding undiscovered in collections that have come down to us. If the reversibility of the text is not mentioned in the title, it is very hard to establish with any certainty. Many poems in the ancient style could clearly accommodate a reverse reading. Thus I am limiting myself here to those formally recognized as reversible poems.

TANG DYNASTY
(618–907)

The Tang Dynasty is rightly considered the golden age of Chinese poetry. The country was unified and lived in peace and prosperity. All the arts—painting, calligraphy, sculpture, architecture—experienced unprecedented developments and poetry evolved toward the so-called modern style, which took into account recent discoveries with regard to phonology: that is, the various tones of the language. These tones were grouped into two categories: the flat tone and the oblique tone, which were alternated according to rules then introduced in poetry, especially in quatrains and octets of five- or seven-syllable lines. The earlier forms of poetry continued nevertheless, and titles often mentioned "the ancient style." During this very open period in which the emperors were also great literati and great collectors—let us remember that Wu Zetian wrote notes on Su Hui—the reversible poem took multiple forms.

Li Shimin: Emperor Taizong (599–649)

As the second emperor of this famous dynasty, Li Shimin composed this circular text, in which one can, it seems, read a thousand poems. But numbers like these no longer impress us!

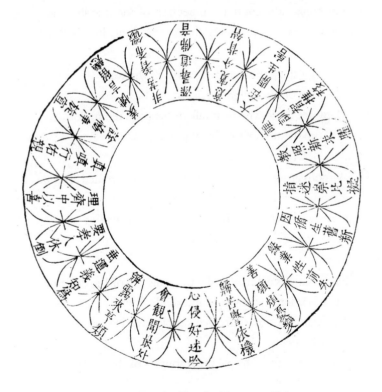

Figure 13.1 Circular Text by Emperor Taizong

One hundred characters are arranged in five concentric circles of twenty characters each. The reader can begin with any of them, following axes that indicate the sequence of the words. The same rhyme can be noted every eleven words and the lines are five syllables in length. Reading will reveal two hundred quatrains. We are far from the reported thousand, but this number very often signifies "many." Among the hundred characters in this system, many of them relate to Buddhism: cause, karma, distraction, worry, wisdom, teaching, doctrine. The distribution of the characters could evoke the "wheel of the law" or the "wheel of a thousand spokes" that symbolizes the continual repetition of the Buddha's doctrine, that "new wisdom" introduced from India along the Silk Road:

Distinguishing the manifest words of the way
The man of pure behavior is just.
Many are those who hear talk of his good reputation
His true nature honors the new wisdom.

Wisdom grows through imitation of the transmitted doctrine
Previous actions favored the spirit of trickery.
Freeing oneself from the external is a fundamental joy
Proclaiming the truth exalts subtlety and depths.

Earlier causes determine the transmission of the doctrine
Great wisdom, a profound and subtle desire.
The manifestation of truth takes pleasure in essential
     schemes
Releasing to the external the resources of the spirit is
     beneficial.

Anonymous: The Hermit of the South Mountains

Here is a square arrangement of forty-nine characters divided into seven lines of seven words:

好處深居近翠嶺
音親邈客侍閒秀
清室邀喜侍吟聳
玉淨喜席歸恣晶
漱聰終闌酒取飛
泉寒陪聚宴歡澗
覓宜檜竹松邊水

Figure 14.1 Square Arrangement of Text

We have already learned that forty-nine characters do not make a poem. So we need to find a way to read it. In fact, this is a matter of a heptasyllabic octet, with a total of fifty-six characters. It is obtained by beginning each line with the last word of the line before it. We encountered this process in the eight poems of the central part of Su Hui's text. The poem begins with the character 寒 *han* (cold), which indicates the category of the chosen rhymes. This word is repeated three times in the poem. The reading ends in the central square, which is not left blank here. In the lower left corner, we find a character 無 *wu* drawn in contours which means "nothing" and is not integrated into the poem. Rather the character allows the poem to function. The reading advances square by square in a spiral following this order:

7/8	9	10	11	12	13	14/15
6	33	34	35/36	37	38	16
5	32	49/50	51	52	39	17
4	31	48	56	53	40	18
3	30	47	55	54	41	19
2	1/29 28	46	45	44	43/42	20
Nothing	27	26	25	24	23	22/21

Figure 14.2 Reading Order of the Square Arrangement of Text

Cold spring, pure jade, clear marvelous sound
Marvelous spot, the secluded dwelling, near and blue-
    tinged, the mountains.
Mountains covered with vegetation, high peaks, springing
    from the falls, water
Water, on its bank's pines, bamboo and cypress bear the cold.

Cold the windows of the hermitage, the relation invites
   his guest
Guest and servant idly sing, take pleasure as they wish.
Pleasure of feasting in each other's company, to the end of
   the happy meal
Happy to come and go, of the wine only a drop remains.

In the reverse reading that begins with the central character, the paired lines also retain the rhyme:

The remaining wine puts them in good form, to come
   and go happy
Happy to feast in company, enjoying a meal together to
   the end is a pleasure.
Pleasure taken singing as they wish, idling, the servant
   and his guest
The guest invited into the relation's house, the empty
   window is cold.
Cold suits cypress and bamboo, beside the pines, water
Water from the falls flows on the peaks, high and covered
   with vegetation, the mountains.
Mountains blue-tinged near the dwelling, marvelous
   secluded spot
Marvelous the sound of clear jade, the spring pure and cold.

In the first reading, the author moves us gradually from the natural setting to inside the house. In the second, we are inside and we see the surrounding landscape through the window that is empty, that is, lacking its oiled paper. We penetrate into the square, then we reemerge from it.

Anonymous (7th Century): The Map on a Hanging Mirror (*Panjiantu*)

There are two words we are familiar with in this title 盤鑒圖 *panjiantu*: "pan" of the pedestal or base, and "tu," map or diagram. This is not surprising when we discover the form of the poem. "Pan jian" refers to a leather belt ornamented with a bronze mirror. The term is associated with a long tradition of exhortation texts that literati-officials drafted in order to warn their superiors against abuses. Some of those exhortations were inscribed on hanging mirrors. Like Su Hui's poem, they were copied out and used as decor. The print reproduced below comes from a mirror cast in 1782 that appears in the collection of the Imperial Palace in Beijing, as indicated by the characters engraved between the volutes that were not part of the original text.

The discovery of this poem is credited to Wang Bo (649–676) when he was traveling in southern China. It is attributed to "a brilliant young woman" known for another poem, on separation, supposedly written when she was seven years old. In this text Wang Bo found qualities of exhortation that made it an equal to works of the past. With its various reading levels it also deserves to be included among the most beautiful examples of the reversible poem.

It is composed of a total of one hundred ninety-two characters and the presence of eight trigrams leads us again to consider numbers. Eight characters adorn the central motif and eight characters appear at the center of the volutes around the perimeter.

Figure 15.1 Print Reproduction of the *panjiantu*[1]

The central flower generates sixteen couplets in lines of four syllables with rhymes. Reading can begin with any character, and then turning toward the right or the left. The arrangement alternates four nouns and four verbs or adjectives. Diametrically opposed words rhyme with one another:

Immaculate snow, pure wave
The moon gleams, the river is clear.

The snow is clear, the river illuminated
The moon is pure, the wave brilliant.

The pure moon gleams in the river
The clear snow makes the wave shine.

The wave is pure, the moon gleams
The river is clear, the snow immaculate...and so on.

A second way of reading, identical to the first, is determined by the eight characters located at the center of the volutes. Diametrically opposed words rhyme with one another and offer sixteen couplets:

Pure light of the sun that shines
The scent of water chestnuts in the lit room.

The sun shines, the light is pure
The room lit, scented water chestnuts.

Water chestnuts in the brilliant light of the sun
Bright room, lit and scented.

In China there is a great tradition of couplets or "parallel maxims." Calligraphed on vertical strips of paper, they are hung from each side of a doorway, attached to the wall on either side of a mirror, or an altar.... It is in its own right a very popular genre. They appear continually in numerous collections, sometimes arranged by themes for every occasion: marriage, the new year, birth....

The third way of reading begins with the hundred seventy-six characters arranged in volutes and allows the reader to decipher forty-eight four-syllable couplets by continuing to the left or to the right. The characters located at the intersections of the volutes—

sixteen in number—are used two times, in different lines. Here are eighty couplets beginning with the word *pian* 篇 (writing, literary composition). In the direction of the reading that goes from left to right, the lines rhyme with *zhi*, and in the opposite direction, they rhyme with *xian*.

The writing is hidden and concise
Its combinations are refined.

The white of ceruse, composing ornaments from it
Exerting itself without reserve to (distinguish) beauty and
  ugliness.

In reconsidering itself so as to combine
In its perfect virtue, the text opens out.

The light that is cast sparkles with brilliance
The figures that spread out manifest the marvelous.
  (figures from the *I Ching*)

First others, then oneself
Read the *Book of Rites*, venerate the *Book of Songs*.

Suspended in the room, the figures are exposed
By opening the case, the light spreads.
  (books used to be arranged in cases, the spreading light
   symbolizes the beneficial teachings drawn from the classics)

The renowned transmission goes back to Antiquity
Its clarity spreads in minuscule quantities.

Solid, it is only the pure stone
From various marks, the worn stone is black.

A row of stars leads to the moon
The water plants agitated, their scent spreads.

To observe the multicolored embroideries of the brocade
Their appearance rivals the ceaseless undulations of the
      water.

Pious thoughts from morning until evening
Maintain respect in the women's quarters.

Empty and full are in harmony in the Way
The network of figures is ordered according to the two
      principles. (that is, *Yin* and *Yang*)

The fog is like sheets of jade
The shadows look like scented branches.

Drive away imperfections, purify what is dirty
Dispel hatred, leave weariness behind.

The lotus through its scent manifests its qualities
The sun in its whiteness is difficult to discern.
      (regarding how difficult it can be to perceive the
      visible when the invisible is so obvious)

By ordering the words, extend the meaning
Their qualities stir us by following their arrangement.

Consider what is ahead, beware of what is behind
The snow is swept away, the clouds dispelled.

Beating its wings, the woodpecker flies off
Reflected or veiled, the words spread.

Along the temples, hair in cicada wings
Eyebrows in blue willow leaves.
> (make-up and hair styles fashionable in this period)

All and little curb aspirations
Venerate what is beautiful, respect what is inferior.

A fresh fish in the beak of a kingfisher
Its shadow crosses the surface of the pond.

The spring divides, the branches of the river spread
Earth waits, heaven regulates.

Extend life, increase longevity
Generations change, time passes.

Caught in the waiting net that gives them a meaning
The many colors separate the words.

Many references to Taoism and the *I Ching* appear in these eighty couplets: the alternation of elements, the flow of time, the complementary nature of full and empty, the illusion of reality.... The net in question in the last couplet refers to a famous phrase from the philosopher Zhuangzi: "The fish caught, forget the net."

Here, it means forgetting the words and their appearance once the meaning is grasped. Do the many colors evoke Su Hui's poem or perhaps this poem was itself in color? Wang Bo makes no mention of it. So let us be content with these eighty couplets in black and white.

NOTE

1. This is a mirror rubbing of the *Panjiantu* taken from *Gugong Cangjing*, Zijincheng chubanshe, 1996, p. 197.

Quan Deyu (759–818) and Pan Mengyang (?)

Quan Deyu enjoyed fame in his lifetime; he was the very model of the state official-literati. He held various government offices—president of the Ministry of Rites, then the Ministry of Justice—and left a vast opus of prose and poetry, but he seems to have lacked true originality. Quan Deyu only figures in the history of literature as a minor writer. He was interested in various poetic forms in fashion during the Six Dynasties period, the reversible text among them. One day he received a quatrain in this form from the poet Pan Mengyang, to which he responded.

By Pan Mengyang:

春日雪　　　　chun ri xue

春梅雜落雪	chun mei za luo xue
發樹幾花開	fa shu ji hua kai
真須盡興飲	zhen xu jin xing yin
仁里願同來	ren li yuan tong lai

Snow One Day in Spring

The plum trees in spring merge with the snow that falls
On the budding trees, how many blossoms open?

It is truly necessary to devote oneself to the pleasure of
   drinking
In such good company, the desire to be together.

*

Coming together, we desire kindly company
Drinking brings joy, all want sincerity.
Open blossoms, on how many trees do they appear?
Snow falls, many-colored plum trees in spring.

Quan Deyu's response:

酒杯春醉好	jiu bei chun zui hao
飛雪晚庭閒	fei xue wan ting xian
久憶同前賞	jiu yi tong qian shang
中林對遠山	zhong lin dui yuan shan

A cup of wine, in spring being drunk is good
Snow that flutters, evening the courtyard is peaceful.
Long recalling our meetings in days gone by
The central forest faces the distant mountains.

*

Mountains in the distance, they face the heart of the forest
Appreciating the past, shared memories are old.
In the peaceful courtyard, evening the snow flutters
Loving drunkenness in spring, a cup of wine.

Lü Dongbin (798–?)

Lü Dongbin is not as well known for the few poems that are included in *The Complete Poems of the Tang* as he is for his Taoist activities. He is no less than one of the eight immortals appearing in that pantheon, so it is fitting that the date of his death remains unknown. The great master of internal alchemy, Lü Dongbin based his technique on the concept of return. He was also the patron saint of brothels, because it seems he excelled in converting prostitutes. It may have been within the context of these activities that he composed two circular inscriptions, both exhortations. The ways of reading them evoke very clearly the idea of the vicious circle...which is necessary to escape at any cost:

Figure 17.1 First Circular Inscription by Lü Dongbin

Although the word "wine" provided in the title does not appear in the text, it is understood in the sixteen couplets: it is because of wine that all these bad things happen.

Exhortation against Wine

Body depraved, country devastated
Minds corrupted, virtue offended.

The body is ravaged, the country corrupted
Minds are offended, virtue depraved.

Country ravaged, minds corrupted
Virtue offended, bodies depraved.

The country is corrupted, minds offended
Virtue is depraved, bodies ravaged.

It corrupts minds, offends virtue
Depraves bodies, ravages the country.

Minds are offended, virtue depraved
The body is ravaged, the country corrupted.

It offends virtue, depraves bodies
Ravages the country, corrupts minds.

Virtue is depraved, the body ravaged
The country is corrupted, minds are offended.

Virtue is offended, minds corrupted
The country is ravaged, bodies depraved.

It offends minds, corrupts the country
Ravages bodies, depraves virtue.

Minds are corrupted, the country ravaged
The body is depraved, virtue offended.

Country corrupted, body ravaged
Virtue depraved, minds offended.

The country is ravaged, the body depraved
Virtue is offended, minds corrupted.

Bodies ravaged, virtue depraved
Minds offended, the country is corrupted.

The body is depraved, virtue offended
Minds are corrupted, the country ravaged.

Virtue depraved, minds offended
Country corrupted, bodies ravaged.

It is not the exhaustion of so many readings that matters, but the feeling that it is impossible to escape this vicious circle, as in the second example:

Figure 17.2 Second Circular Inscription by Lü Dongbin

Exhortation against Lust

It makes one forget authenticity, it corrupts vital energy
It offends minds, depraves aspirations.

Authenticity becomes corrupted, vital energy is offended
Minds are depraved, aspirations are forgotten.

Vital energy corrupted, minds offended
Aspirations depraved, authenticity forgotten.

Vital energy is offended, minds depraved
Aspirations are forgotten, authenticity corrupted

...and so on

These exhortations are constructed according to the same pattern: alternating noun and verb, diametrically opposed rhymes, and parallelism within each couplet. The master Taoist needed only to replace the keyword, and the incantatory litany was set in motion.

Pi Rixiu (834–883) and Lu Guimeng (?–881)

Pi Rixiu, born in present-day Hubei, went to Suzhou in 869 to take up an official prefectorial post. There he encountered Lu Guimeng, a poet deeply immersed in Taoism, and the two men struck up a friendship. They collaborated on many works, more than three hundred of which survive. Pi Rixiu wrote the preface to one of their shared collections. There he laid out his vision of the evolution of poetry since Antiquity. Based on tonal alternation and parallelism, the modern forms that culminated in the masterpieces of the height of the Tang were well established by the time Pi Rixiu appeared on the literary scene one hundred years later. Perhaps he was seeking something more innovative in the *Poems of Varied Forms*. He even attempted to trace their lineage beginning from the *Book of Songs*. Thus he defined twenty-two poetic forms, citing the first known author and the first words of the poem of reference. The reversible poem was included in this list; a translation of the relevant passage appears at the beginning of this book. Pi Rixiu concludes his preface with these words: "Ah! From ancient poems to regular poems, from regular poems to varied forms, the Way of poetry is thus achieved!"

The history of literature does not prove him entirely right. Following regular poems in the forms of the modern style came the formidable fashion of poems to be sung, *ci*, which developed especially during the Song dynasty. Contact with foreign peoples, notably through the Silk Road but also during the "Barbarian" invasions, favored the introduction of new instruments and new music that influenced all poetic creation, offering new rhyme schemes. Varied forms and reversible poems continued to be practiced, but never became a major trend, as Pi Rixiu had hoped. The two friends tried their hands at those diverse forms. They left two reversible poems that are seven-syllable octets.

By Lu Guimeng:

曉起即事寄皮襲美　　　xiao qi ji shi ji pi xi mei

平波落月吟閑景	ping bo luo yue yin xian jing
暗幌浮煙思起人	an huang fu yan si qi ren
清露曉垂花謝半	qing lu xiao chui hua xie ban
遠風微動惠抽新	yuan feng wei dong hui chou xin
城荒上處樵童小	cheng huang shang chu qiao tong xiao
石蘚分來宿鷺馴	shi xian fen lai su lu xun
晴寺野尋同去好	qing si ye xun tong qu hao
古碑苔字細書勻	gu bei tai zi xi shu yun

Up at Dawn to go about his Business, Addressed to Pi Rixui

Water calm, moon setting, celebrating this peaceful
　　landscape
Dark curtain of drifting fog, thinking of the man who
　　rises.
Clear dew at dawn, it drops on blossoms nearly withered
Distant wind, light, it stirs the orchids once again in bud.
At the highest point of the fallow land, on the rampart,
　　the young woodcutter seems small

Lichen on stones, one after another familiar egrets arrive
     to pass the night.
In the sunlit spot, the monastery, to find it in the country,
     it would be good to go together
Moss-covered characters on the old stela, fine regular writing.

*

Regular writing, refined characters, the moss-covered stela
     is ancient
We like leaving together in search of the monastery, in the
     sunlit spot.
Familiar egrets come to pass the night, sharing stones
     covered with lichen
The small child, there where wood is cut, climbs the
     barren rampart.
Orchids newly out are stirring, light wind from the distance.
Half fallen, blossoms hang, the dew of dawn is clear.
The man thinks first of drifting fog like a dark curtain
Peaceful landscape, celebrating the moon, waves subside,
     calmly.

By Pi Rixui:

和陸秀才曉起　　　　he lu xiu cai xiao qi

孤煙曉起初原曲　　　gu yan xiao qi chu yuan qu
碎樹微分半浪中　　　sui shu wei fen ban lang zhong
湖後釣筒移夜雨　　　hu hou diao tong yi ye yu
竹傍磅眠幾側晨風　　　zhu bang mian ji ce chen feng
圖梅帶潤輕沾墨　　　tu mei dai run qing zhan mo

畫蘇經蒸半失紅   hua su jing zheng ban shi hong
無事有杯持永日   wu shi you bei chi yong ri
共君惟好隱牆東   gong jun wei hao yin qiang dong

In Response to "Up at Dawn" by Lu Guimeng

A solitary mist rises at dawn, it begins by winding into the
plain
Broken trees hardly visible in the midst of waves.
Behind the lake, fishing hook and rod are moved with the
night rain
Beside my headrest, bamboo are flattened by the dawn
wind.
Plum trees, as in a drawing, seem wet, lightly saturated
with ink
Perilla, as in a painting, its many veins have nearly lost
their red color.
Without anything to do, having a cup, holding it the
whole day
It is with you alone that I love to hide behind the wall, to
the east.

*

At the eastern wall, hidden lovers, it is only with you that I
share them
All day long I hold a cup, is there something to do or not?
The red has lost half its color, painting of veined perilla
Saturated with lightly moistened ink, drawing of plum
trees.
Dawn wind strikes my pillow slantwise, I sleep beside
bamboo

Rain moves the rod when fishing in the lake behind.
In the midst of waves, fragile trees break into pieces
On the winding plain dawn begins to break, a solitary mist.

SONG DYNASTY
NORTHERN SONG (960–1127)
SOUTHERN SONG (1127–1279)

About fifty years separate the end of the Tang dynasty from the beginning of the Song dynasty, a period in which five dynasties plus some ten realms shared power. As I have found only one poem dating from this time, I am including it at the beginning of this chapter on the Song dynasty.

Xu Yin (Five Dynasties)

閨情

gui qing

飛書一幅錦回文	fei shu yi fu jin hui wen
恨寫深情寄雁來	hen xie shen qing ji yan lai
機上月殘香閣掩	ji shang yue can xiang ge yan
樹梢煙淡綠窗開	shu shao yan dan lü chuang kai
霏霏雨罷歌終曲	fei fei yu ba ge zhong qu
漠漠雲深酒滿杯	mo mo yun shen jiu man bei
舊日幾人行問蔔	jiu ri ji ren xing wen bu
徽音相忘倚高臺	hui yin xiang wang yi gao tai

Feelings in the Women's Suite

Flying letter, text on the strip of brocade returns
Written regrets, deep feelings, sent with wild geese.
On the loom the setting moon, the pavilion of scents is
    closed
In treetops light mist, the green window is open.
Rain that was falling heavily stops, singing ends the tune
Scattered clouds thicken, wine fills the cup.
Day of return, how many of those who leave consult the
    fates?
Good news, they wish it for one another leaning out from
    the high terrace.

*

On the terrace leaning from heights, hoping for news
The fates consulted to learn what day the man who left
    will return.
The cup is full of dark wine, clouds disperse
At the end of the piece, song breaks off, rain falls heavily.
The window open, green fades, mist in the treetops
The pavilion closed, scents drift away, the moon rises over
    the loom.
Wild geese that arrive send feelings, regrets written with
    depth
The strip of brocade to be read reversibly, a letter is sent.

Qian Weizhi (942–1014)

From a collection entitled *Ninety Reversible and Circular Linking Poems of Wu and Yue* (*Wuyue huiwen shoudai lianhuanshi jiushi shou*) attributed to Qian Weizhi, the *Complete Poems of the Song* retained only six texts. They all fall into the varied forms category and bear the same title because they are formal variations on a single subject: "Climbing the Pavilion of Great Compassion on a Spring Day."

春城滿望	chun cheng man wang
曉閣閒登	xiao ge xian deng
塵銷霽景	chen xiao ji jing
定出真僧	ding chu zhen seng
人懷遠思	ren huai yuan si
檻憑危層	jian ping wei ceng
因圓果證	yin yuan guo zheng
勝境斯興	sheng jing si xing

The town in spring is a satisfying sight
The pavilion at dawn, I climb it idly.
Dust disappears, landscape in the sunlit spot
Peacefully departs a virtuous monk.
The man nurtures distant thoughts
The railing protects the upper level.
Acts accomplished, recompense is assured

The transcendent state thus begins.
(or: the remarkable site thus appears, in both cases, an
    allusion to Buddhist enlightenment)

*

Enthusiasm thus surpasses the site
Awakening is achieved through the perfection of acts.
The upper level is high, I lean against the railing
Distant thoughts languishing for someone.
The monk is virtuous, he leaves to find peace
The sunlit spot in the landscape dispels dust.
I climb to the calm pavilion at dawn
I contemplate the whole town in spring.

Qian Weizhi composed two poems in a circular arrangement,
allowing the reader to begin with any word and move in one
direction or the other. We can thus decipher forty pentasyllabic
quatrains with crossed rhymes. The eight that follow represent a
sampling. The reader is free to imagine other possibilities.

In the distant closeness of sky, the bluish kiosk
Moonlight gathers peacefully on the shades.
Cold of the penetrating fog, evening shelter
Mountains dusted with snow, pavilion in the cloud break.

In the blue sky, the kiosk peacefully gathers
By the moon's light the cold shade is penetrated.
Evening mist, the mountainous shelter only a point
In the bright snow, the distant pavilion seems near.

Figure 20.1 First Circular Poem by Qian Weizhi

Penetrating mist, evening the mountainous shelter
Snow scattered, pavilion bright in the distance.
Near the sky, the peaceful blue kiosk
Receiving the moon, the bright shade is cold.

Mountains like a point, snow lights the pavilion
Distant and close, sky turns the kiosk blue.
Peacefully receiving the moon, the shades shine
Cold penetrates the shelter in the misty evening.

Snow punctuates the mountainous shelter
Evening mist penetrates cold shades.
Brilliant moon on the peaceful kiosk
Blue sky, near and distant pavilion.

Evening, like a shelter, mist penetrating and cold
The shade lit up by the moon that peacefully gathers.
The kiosk blue in the sky, near and distant
The pavilion bright in snow that punctuates the mountains.

Cold shades receive the brilliant moon
Peaceful kiosk, blue sky is near.
Distant pavilion, bright snow punctuates it
Mountainous shelter, evening mist penetrates it.

Near and distant, the pavilion in bright snow
Mountains, like a point, shelter evening mist.
Penetrating cold, on the shades shines the moon
Surrounded and peaceful, kiosk in the blue sky.

This circular linkage is not a mere technical feat. It conveys the author's extreme sensitivity to nature, which might seem static at nightfall in the cold and mist. In fact, it is animated by the subtle but constant process of change—the key to the universe. The author offers us a pure example of impressionist poetry. A second circular poem leads us into new kaleidoscopic combinations. Three representative quatrains follow.

A temple in the distance, vapors disperse in curls
The canopy in the sunlit spot supports the fragrant tree.
The courtyard is calm, song embellishes the dawn
Light curtain, the enveloping mist is scented.

Canopy rippling in the sunlit spot, the tree leans against it
In the courtyard full of scents, silent song of the flowers.

Curtain of dawn, light veil of mist
Scented temple, in the distance disperse vapors.

Light curtain, flowered song of the dawn
Silent courtyard, the fragrant trees lean there.
Canopy in the sunlit spot, vapors in curls disperse
Temple in the distance, the scented mist veils it.

...and so on.

Figure 20.2 Second Circular Poem by Qian Weizhi

Sun Mingfu (992–1057) and Pei Yu (?)

Two texts bearing the identical title, "In Imitation of the Embroidered Diagram," allow us to conjecture that their authors knew one another. The ways of reading are also similar: each text is read beginning from the upper left and following zigzags to the center where it continues following the same movement to the exterior to link up finally with the large characters, which are read beginning from the upper left and revolving toward the center.

In the poem by Pei Yu, this reading generates one long poem of seventy-six heptasyllabic lines. If it draws inspiration from the story of Su Hui, its style also recalls the popular version of the handkerchief that circulated in Shaanxi (Figures 21.1 and 21.2).

> Weaving the brocade, weaving the brocade, once again
>   weaving the brocade
> Alone facing the autumn lamp at the point of forgetting
>   repose.
> One character woven, a thousand tears follow
> In the depths of night poured in vain on the embroidered
>   headrest.
> Woven, I will send it to the man who is at the border
> I do not want the master now to forget the body of his
>   wife.
> But I fear for the wife's life, what a sorry fate

Figure 21.1 In Imitation of the Embroidered Diagram (1)

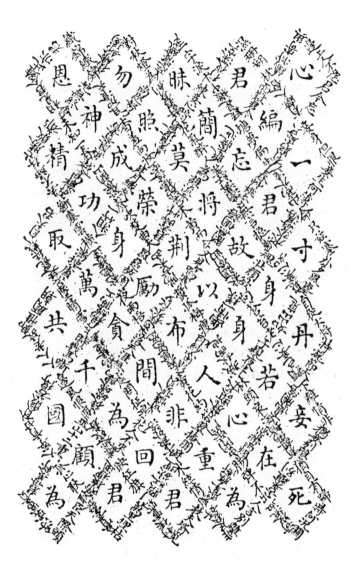

Figure 21.2 In Imitation of the Embroidered Diagram (2)

And worse still beyond the passes (of the Great Wall)
    where the winds of dust are blowing hard.
Since the great general holds the flag of authority
In the empire, feelings of separation are not only for the wife.
After the separation there will be the moment of return
Under what circumstances at the pass flowed the river of
    blood?
People say that separation does not merit melancholy
They prefer to explain that my husband seeks a feudal title.
Over six thousand li snow and fog hide dried bones
The solitary official grew old at the borders of heaven
    (and earth).
Floating clouds of happiness and wealth, minister without
    talent
Worth more the simple man, poor and obscure.
If each must grow old in the country of his birth
I desire only that the emperor put an end to the war.
Since my husband left without returning
Of his life or death, success or failure, I no longer know
    anything.
Suddenly in spring a missive, pleasant news
Red with confusion, I go to the mirror to paint my
    eyebrows.
Fragrance of blossoms, the drunk person sleeps, it is not
    yet dawn
A dream at the edge of the pond, spring grasses emerge.
Peach and pear trees do not speak but they summon souls
The vigor of youth would like to last as the lichen do.
At midnight the cuckoo at the height of the forest is
    grieved

Apple trees in clumps under rain and mist blossom.

The green gate closed, overgrown, protects the courtyard
at noon

From the other side of the shade, blossoms fall, no one
comes.

Butterflies make the most of the end of spring, many
bustling about

Partridge cry, the planted weeping willows turn green.

From the other side of the river, listening nostalgically to
people gathering lotus

The sound of the bamboo flute that plays an air of Chu.

When my husband left, the grass and trees were yellow

And again today I see the buzzing fireflies of the cold.

The lone plum tree casts its thin silhouette on the window
screen

I meditate sadly, the autumn rains persist.

In the setting sun the old tree detests the west wind

In the ancient garden, night rain falls on the sterculia
trees.

At the sky's borders not a place to ask after migrating
geese

What a shame to appear ungrateful, the young people
were engaged.

Sound of the reed flute breaks off, autumn at the Great Wall

In both places intimate feelings are equally melancholy.

Leaning sadly in the hollow of the railing with no one to
talk to

Red leaves fill the canal, for whom does it flow?

Frost forms on the stone for beating (laundry), moon in
the empty courtyard

Weaving a coat, I wish to send it beyond the mountains of
the pass.
From the high pavilion the view is blocked, cloud bank to
the marches (of the empire)
Reeds in blossom that cover the ground collapse under
bright snow.
In this moment war horses neigh, barbarian customs
I fear that Wu is separated by twelve mountain ranges.
Solitary heart tormented, the gibbon cries in the central
plain
Everywhere the shadow of the (punitive) expeditions flag,
a red spot.
Heart overflowing with feelings, I want to tune the icy
string (of the instrument)
Hand echoing the despair, I cannot manage to play.
Since ancient times who is grieved by separation
At the bottom of the steps in the dark, orchids lose their
color.
The concubine's heart is like high mountains
The concubine's heart is like waters that murmur.
Mountains are high, waters withdraw, there is one farthest
point
Only the man who departed risks confronting the
difficulty of it.
The husband now doubts that it is a matter of silk made
on the loom
The concubine secretly hopes to see again the husband
who bears the sword.
I persist in thinking of it still and I add courses (as an offering)
Heaven and earth can see one another without end.

The husband left that place today and received a favor
  (from the emperor)
The husband's heart does not act against his conscience, a
  bit of cinnabar (loyalty).
The concubine dies for the husband, the husband for the
  country
In common they chose the mind in accordance with the
  classics.
The man himself if he is alive will again remember for-
  mer things
A thousand, ten thousand merits rendered, but no one
  forgets the past.
The body and mind do not honor a life of greed
In this world I strive for modesty and virtue.

Mei Chuang (?)

There is no information available to us on this author who chose the theme of the four seasons for a series of four reversible poems, the premise of that form, more than all others, conforming to the idea of cyclical alternation.

春	chun
畫永春庭邃	zhou yong chun ting sui
雙飛燕隔簾	shuang fei yan ge lian
袖隨簾捲翠	xiu sui lian juan cui
時見玉纖纖	shi jian yu xian xian

Spring

The day is prolonged in spring, in the depth of the
    courtyard
Flying in pairs, the swallows behind the bamboo shade.
The sleeve follows the shade that rolls up, blue-tinged
At this moment appears all the delicacy of a jade.
    (the arm of a pretty woman)

*

When a delicate jade appears
Bluish roller, the shade follows the sleeve.
Behind the shade, swallows fly in pairs
In the deep courtyard, spring prolongs the day.

夏　　　　　　xia

曲澗跳珠碎　　qu jian tiao zhu sui
叢山疊翠濃　　cong shan die cui nong
竹新敷影薄　　zhu xin fu ying bo
閒看倚枝筇　　xian kan yi zhi qiong

Summer

The torrent enclosed, winding, leaps, shattering its pearls
　　of water
Massive mountains rise in tiers, emerald and dense.
The bamboo, young, give off a light shadow
Idly I gaze, leaning on a bamboo cane.

*

Leaning against the bamboo poles, I gaze idly
Light shade spreads over the young bamboo.
Deep emerald, the terraced mountains close in
Shattered pearls leap in the twists and turns of the torrent.

A single word, "bamboo," in English and French is used to
translate two Chinese words, zhu (bamboo), and qiong (the gnarled
bamboo from which canes are made).

秋　　　　　　qiu

小雨涼添夜　　xiao yu liang tian ye
蘭芬潤襲衣　　lan fen run xi yi
曉屏山曲曲　　xiao ping shan qu qu
長若夢思歸　　chang ruo meng si gui

Autumn

A fine rain with its coolness fills the night
The scent of orchids permeates clothing.
The folds at dawn of the distant mountains
Long in dream, thinking of coming back.

*

Thoughts of return in dream continue
Remote, the mountainous shelter illuminated.
Clothes become permeated with fragrant orchids
The night intensifies, a cold rain, fine.

冬	dong
曲經穿叢密	qu jing chuan cong mi
香清為客來	xiang qing wei ke lai
玉梢梢外雪	yu shao shao wai xue
苔古暈疏梅	tai gu yun shu mei

Winter

A winding path crosses thick groves
Light scents for the coming of a guest.
Rustlings of jade, the snow outside
The ancient mosses, spots on plum trees in the distance.

*

Plum trees in the distance like spots on old mosses
Beyond the snow the rustlings of jade.
The guest who arrives bears a light scent
Thick groves through which winds the path.

Four other reversible poems by Mei Chuang have come down to us:

秋江寫望　　　　　qiu jiang xie wang

寒江慕泊小舟輕　　han jiang mu bo xiao zhou qing
白鷺樓煙叢葦鳴　　bai lü lou yan cong wei ming
寬望遠空浮湛碧　　kuan wang yuan kong fu zhan bi
老蟾驚玉弄秋清　　lao chan jing yu nong qiu qing

Describing What I See on the River in Autumn

On the cold river at sunset a small light boat drops anchor
White egrets at the pavilion in the mist, gather in reeds to
　　sing.
As far as the eye can see in the distant void drifts deep azure
Old toad frightens the sky, sowing trouble in autumnal
　　light.

*

Autumn pure as jade, the old toad is disturbed
Depth of azure drifting in the void, the view gets lost in
　　the distance.
Singing in misty groves of reeds, egrets from the pavilion,
　　white
The small light boat drops anchor at sunset on the cold
　　river.

The old toad is an allusion to the lunar toad who, according to tradition, lives on the moon and swallows it during eclipses.

西湖戲書二首   xi hu xi shu er shou

蜿蜿翠麓時煙漲   wan wan cui lu shi yan zhang
灩灩金波夜月澄   yan yan jin bo ye yue deng
樽酒具時隨興遣   zun jiu ju shi sui xing qian
景多逢處曲欄憑   jing duo feng chu qu lan ping

Two Poems Composed on West Lake for Amusement

The bluish foot of the mountain ripples, by the moment
    mist rises
Golden waves shine, night of pure moon.
When wine cups are set out, letting oneself go to
    exhilaration
There are many shadows in the meeting place, leaning
    against the gnarled gate.

*

At the resting gate of this secluded place, many shadows
    meet
Letting go to exhilaration with the passing hours,
    preparing wine cups.
The pure moon on nocturnal waves, shining like gold
Mist rising at the foot of the mountains, bluish by the
    moment, ripples.

雲巢望斷望西湖   yun chao wang duan wang xi hu
竹護梅藏隱士居   zhu hu mei cang yin shi ju
芳草綠深春盎盎   fang cao lü shen chun ang ang
客來同攬一山孤   ke lai tong lan yi shan gu

From the mountain hut, the distant view is interrupted,
   contemplating West Lake
Protected by bamboo, hidden among plum trees, the
   hermit's dwelling.
Scented grass, deep green, spring so exuberant
The guest arrives, together let us take in the sight of a
   solitary mountain.

*

Gushan, perceived suddenly by the guests arriving together
What exuberance, full spring, scented green grass.
The inhabitant hides, plum trees protect the bamboo
West of the lake, the view is interrupted by contemplating
   banked clouds.

West Lake is a proper noun, designating the famous lake of
Hangzhou. In the reverse reading, it changes into "west of the
lake," becoming a common noun. The same is true of Gushan, or
Solitary Mountain, a single peak that dominates the lake. According to reading direction, place names are thus transformed into
simple qualifier-qualified combinations.

The other poem Mei Chuan left to us is a *ci*, that is, a poem to
be sung. The repertoire of tunes for this genre was limited to eight
hundred seventy melodies. Each tune determined the metrics of
the text, the pattern of tonal alternation, and the rhyme. The *ci*
differs from other poems because of its heterometry. Unlike other
poems, the number of syllables per line can vary within a single
poem. The poet had to adapt the number of syllables to a pre-existing melodic pattern. Titles generally mention the chosen tune.

While the texts have been preserved, the music itself has unfortunately disappeared because it was not written down.

西江月泛湖	xi jiang yue fan hu
過雨輕風弄柳	guo yu qing feng nong liu
湖東映日春煙	hu dong ying ri chun yan
晴蕪平水遠連天	qing wu ping shui yuan lian tian
隱隱飛翻舞燕	yin yin fei fan wu yan
燕舞翻飛隱隱	yan wu fan fei yin yin
天連遠水平蕪	tian lian yuan shui ping wu
晴煙春日映東湖	qing yan chun ri ying dong hu
柳弄風輕雨過	liu nong feng qing yu guo

Generally in a sung poem, the reverse reading becomes an integral part of the text, as in this example. Here, only one character changes lines.

To the Tune of the Moon on West River:
Sailing on the Lake

Rain over, a light wind stirs the willows
East of the lake, reflected sun, spring mist.
In the sunlit spot, wild grasses and calm waters in the
    distance merge with sky
Many are flying, wheeling, the swallows.
Swallows dance, wheel, numerous
Sky merges with distant waters, flattened grasses.
In the sunlit spot, misty spring, the sun reflected in East Lake
Willows play with the wind, the light rain passes.

Liu Chang (1019–1068)

A prose writer and historian specializing in the classics, Liu Chang maintained relationships with the great writers of his time, Sima Guang and Ouyang Xiu, who considered him a man of high culture. Among his many writings are two reversible poems, one of which is this quatrain in regular style, comprised of two parallel couplets:

雨後	yu hou
綠水池光冷	lü shui chi guang leng
青苔砌色寒	qing tai qi se han
竹深啼鳥亂	zhu shen ti niao luan
庭暗落花殘	ting an luo hua can

After the Rain

Blue-green water, icy light of the pond
Green mosses, cold color of the steps.
In the depth of bamboo, singing birds are stirring
In the darkness of the courtyard, fallen blossoms wilt.

*

Wilted blossoms fall in the dark courtyard
Stirring birds sing in dense bamboo.
Cold color, the mossy steps are green
Icy light, pond water is blue-green.

Kong Pingzhong (11th century)

Kong Pingzhong held various official governmental positions and was also dismissed from government many times. He left a vast amount of work, compiled with that of his two brothers in the voluminous *Collection of the Three Kongs of Qingjiang*. In it appear many poems of varied forms, among them five reversible poems. In these quatrains, the author follows strict rules of tonal alternation and masterfully exploits reversals in meaning as well as the polysemous nature of the characters.

題纖錦璿圖回文五絕　　ti zhi jin xuan tu hui wen wu jue

紅窗小泣低聲怨　　hong chuang xiao qi di sheng yuan
永夕春風鬥帳空　　yong xi chun feng dou zhang kong
中酒落花飛絮亂　　zhong jiu luo hua fei xu luan
曉鶯啼破夢匆匆　　xiao ying ti po meng cong cong

Five Reversible Poems on the Theme of the Brocade of the Armillary Sphere

At the red window quiet tears, in a hushed voice
　　a complaint
Long night, spring wind, the sky of bed is empty.
Wilted blossoms fall in the wine, down flies here and there
At dawn orioles sing, shattering the dream in their haste.

*

Quick, quick, the dream comes to an end, orioles
    singing at dawn
Down pell-mell and blossoms flying that fall in the wine.
Empty curtain in north wind, night lingers on
Plaintive voice, silent tears, small red window.

稀草露如郎薄幸	xi cao lu ru lang bao xing
亂花飛似妾情多	luan hua fei si qie qing duo
歸鴻見處揮珠淚	gui hong jian chu hui zhu lei
語燕聞時斂翠娥	yu yan wen shi lian cui e

Dew on the sparse grass is like rare favors from the
    master
Blossoms that fly in all directions are like the wife's many
    feelings.
Seeing the returning wild geese come to rest, she dries her
    tears
When she hears swallows singing, the lovely woman lures
    them to her.

*

When she knits her brows, she hears swallows
    singing
The tears that form dried, she sees wild geese return.
With her many feelings, the wife resembles blossoms that
    fly in all directions
With his rare favors, the husband is like scattered dew on
    the grass.

In the first reading, the last two words of the poem, *cui e*, mean a beautiful woman, a beauty, and in the opposite direction, *e cui*, they designate long, delicate, black eyebrows.

琴絃斷續愁兼恨	qin xian duan xu chou jian hen
嶺水分流西複東	ling shui fen liu xi fu dong
深院小扉紅日落	shen yuan xiao fei hong ri luo
繡窗閒倚更誰同	xiu chuang xian yi geng shui tong

Strings of the lute do not stop, sadness is mixed with
    resentment
Water from the summits spreads as it flows, west returns
    to east.
In the inner courtyard, by the entrance's small door, the
    red sun sets
Leaning at the window of the women's suite, idle, with
    whom to be together again?

*

With whom to lean again, carefree, at the carved window?
The setting sun reddens the entrance's door, small inner
    courtyard.
From east toward west again flows and spreads the water
    on the summits
Resentment and sadness endure, lute with broken strings.

In the first line *duan* means to break, *xu* to continue, and *duanxu* to continue intermittently. In reverse, *duan* is read with *xian* to make *duanxian*, broken strings. To break a lute string is a metaphor meaning that a man is losing his woman.

參橫霽色天沉水　　can heng ji se tian chen shui
鳥宿寒枝竹銷煙　　niao su han zhi zhu xiao yan
衾惹舊香清夜半　　qin re jiu xiang qing ye ban
淚凝殘燭畫堂前　　lei ning can zhu hua tang qian

Rising from east to west in the azure, sky laden with water
Birds nest on cold branches, in the bamboo, mist
　　dissipates.
The chamber exudes old scents in the midst of the clear
　　night
Fixed tears of the candle burned before the hall of
　　paintings.

*

In the front hall, the painted candle goes out, fixing its tears
Midnight, pure scents, as in the past, cloud the chamber.
Mist dissipates in bamboo branches, in the cold, birds nest.
Water floods the color of the sky, cloud break rises from
　　east to west.

寒信霜風秋葉黃　　han xin shuang feng qiu ye huang
冷燈殘月照空床　　leng deng can yue zhao kong chuang
看君寄意傳文錦　　kan jun ji yi chuan wen jin
字字愁縈惹斷腸　　zi zi chou ying re duan chang

Wind and frost announce the cold, autumn leaves turn
　　yellow
Icy star, the setting moon lights the empty bed.
Out of consideration for the master, conveying one's
　　thoughts, sending an ornate brocade

Word after word, sadness turns in all directions, breaking
the heart.

*

The heart broken prompts turning in circles, sadness in all
the words
Text on a brocade conveys feelings, sending it to the
master, let him read it.
Empty bed, brilliant moon, the extinguished lantern is icy
Yellow leaves, autumn wind, the time of frost is cold.

In the first line *xin* combined with *han* means the announce-
ment of the winter cold. Combined with *shuang* in the reverse
reading, *shuangxin* means the period of frost.

Wang Anshi (1021–1086)

Wang Anshi served as a government official. Philosopher and poet, turned prime minister, he had the ambitions of a great reformer and attempted a complete overhaul of the state financial system. He also wanted to reform the army, education...disrupting the whole of society through his measures and giving each segment the impression of being wronged. Thus he incurred the enmity of the rich and the wrath of the poor. Under pressure from his many opponents, Wang Anshi was forced to renounce his reforms, which no doubt gave him time to devote himself to poetry.

無題三首	wu ti san shou
碧蕪平野曠	bi wu ping ye kuang
黃菊晚村深	huang ju wan cun shen
客倦留酣飲	ke juan liu han yin
身閒累苦吟	shen xian lei ku yin

Three Untitled Poems

Green grass in the midst of the countryside, deserted
Yellow chrysanthemums, evening, isolated village.
Weary, the guest remains to drink his fill
Body idle, tired he composes with difficulty.

*

Singing of suffering tires an idle body.
Drinking his fill, the guest remains weary.
Secluded village, evening chrysanthemums are yellow
Barren country, the short grass is green.

夢長隨永漏   meng chang sui yong lou
吟苦雜疏鐘   yin ku za shu zhong
動蓋荷風勁   dong gai he feng jing
霑裳菊露濃   zhan shang ju lu nong

The dream persists in keeping with the perennial water
     clock
The sad song merges with the distant bell.
Canopy stirred, a fierce wind in the lotus
Drenched skirt, heavy dew on the chrysanthemums.

*

Heavy dew, drenched chrysanthemum petals
Fierce wind, the lotus corollas stirred.
Bell in the distance merges with sad song
Water clock goes on and on conforming to the dream that
     persists.

迸月川魚躍   beng yue chuan yu yue
開雲嶺鳥翻   kai yun ling niao fan
徑斜荒草惡   jing xie huang cao e
台廢冶花繁   tai fei ye hua fan

Leaping after the moon, fish in the river jump
Splitting the clouds, birds on the peaks flit about.

Sloping path, wild grasses obstruct it
Terrace in ruins, ravishing blossoms proliferate there.

*

Many blossoms adorn the terrace in ruins
Weeds invade the sloping path.
Flitting birds, clouds over the peaks break up
Jumping fish, the moon in the river appears.

Wang Anshi wrote this octet as well:

客懷	ke huai
泊雁鳴深渚	bo yan ming shen zhu
收霞落晚川	shou xia luo wan chuan
柝隨風斂陣	tuo sui feng lian zhen
樓映月低弦	lou ying yue di xian
漠漠汀帆轉	mo mo ting fan zhuan
幽幽岸火燃	you you an huo ran
壑危通細路	he wei tong xi lu
溝曲繞平田	gou qu rao ping tian

Thoughts of a Traveler

Wild geese at rest squawk on a secluded island
Receiving the pink clouds of the falling evening, a river.
The clapping of the night watch carried by the wind, the
    shower passes.
The pavilion reflects the moon, its quarter tilts.
On the silent bank a sail beats
On the distant shore a fire flares.

Great peril in taking the narrow path
The twists and turns of the channel unwind all around the
     leveled fields.

*

Flat fields skirt around the winding ravine
The narrow path surmounts the danger.
A fire crackles on the distant shore
A sail floats on the silent bank.
The low quarter moon is reflected in the pavilion
The shower checks the wind, one night watch follows
     another.
On the river, evening, red clouds that gather there fall
On the secluded island squawk wild geese at rest.

Su Dongpo (1036–1101)

Wang Anshi's contemporary, Su Dongpo was violently opposed to his reforms. As a government official, Su Dongpo experienced alternating periods of favor and disgrace throughout his career. His poetic and calligraphic works make him one of the most engaging and important figures of the Song and of the whole history of Chinese literature. In his lifetime, he already enjoyed immense popularity. Imbued with Taoist philosophy, his poetry manifests great sensitivity, but he was not averse to the inspiration offered by a cup of wine. He took an interest in very diverse forms, which included the reversible poem.

春機滿織回文錦	chun ji man zhi hui wen jin
粉淚揮殘露井桐	fen lei hui can lu jing tong
人遠寄情書字小	ren yuan ji qing shu zi xiao
柳絲低月晚庭空	liu si di yue wan ting kong

In spring the loom never stops weaving, reversible brocade
Make-up ruined, wiping one's tears, a sterculia beside the
    well.
To the man far away, to share one's feelings, characters on
    the letter are small
Willow twigs, low moon, evening the courtyard is empty.

*

In the empty courtyard, the evening moon leans over the
 silky willows
Small characters relating feelings, sent to the man far
 away.
Well with a sterculia where make-up is revealed, ruined by
 wiped tears
Text on brocade through the weaving shuttles invades the
 loom in spring.

紅牋短寫空深恨	hong jian duan xie kong shen hen
錦句新翻欲斷腸	jin ju xin fan yu duan chang
風葉落殘驚夢蝶	feng ye luo can jing meng die
戍邊回雁寄情郎	shu bian hui yan ji qing lang

On red paper writing briefly of deep and vain regrets
Through new reversals of the lines of brocade, wishing to
 break the heart.
In wind withered leaves fall, frightening the butterfly of
 dreams
At the borders returning wild geese convey feelings to the
 master.

*

Feelings toward the master are confided to wild geese
 who return to the borders
The butterfly of dreams, frightened, disappears, wind
 making the leaves fall.
The broken heart can interpret the new lines of the brocade
Regrets are deep, written in vain a short letter on red
 paper.

Red paper is used for calligraphing poems or parallel sentences for decorating houses, with red being the color of happiness. The third line is an illusion to the Taoist philosopher Zhuangzi, who confessed to not knowing if he was Zhuangzi dreaming he was a butterfly or a butterfly dreaming he was Zhuangzi.

Under the title, "Memories of a Dream," Su Dongpo composed two other reversible quatrains, accompanied by a preface:

On the fifteenth day of the twelfth month, during the period of the Great Snow, when the weather began to clear up, I dreamed that someone heated water for brick tea in the melted snow and that a lovely woman sang while drinking what remained of it. In my dream, I composed a poem, and in waking, I remembered the first line: "Scattered drops of abundant blossoms, cast on the blue tunic." The meaning refers to the story of Feiyan spitting flowers, and I thus continued with these quatrains.

記夢回文二首   **ji meng hui wen er shou**

酡顏玉碗捧纖纖   tuo yan yu wan peng xian xian
亂點餘花唾碧衫   luan dian yu hua tuo bi shan
歌咽水雲凝靜院   ge yan shui yun ning jing yuan
夢驚松雪落空岩   meng jing song xue luo kong yan

Two Reversible Poems in Memory of a Dream

Rosy cheeks holding a bowl with her two delicate hands
Scattered drops of abundant blossoms, cast on the blue
    tunic.
Song stifled, clouds full of water condense over the still
    courtyard
Fearing in the dream that snow falls from pines into
    hollows in the rocks.

*

In the hollow of the rocks falls snow, pines disturb the
 dream.
Over the still courtyard form clouds, (the sound of) water
 drowns the song.
Blue tunic, blossoms cast pell-mell in abundant drops
Delicately holding a bowl in two hands, her jade cheeks
 turn pink.

Zhao Feiyan whom Su Dongpo mentions was the concubine
who became an empress during the reign of Emperor Cheng of
the Han. Su Hui referred to Zhao Feiyan in her poem. The anec-
dote in question recounts how one day, in the company of a favor-
ite courtesan, she inadvertently spit on her sleeve. The courtesan
said that the sprayed brown sleeve was like a stone covered with
blossoms!

空花落盡酒傾缸　　kong hua luo jin jiu qing gang
日上山融雪漲江　　ri shang shan rong xue zhang jiang
紅焙淺甌新火活　　hong bei qian ou xin huo huo
龍團小碾鬥晴窗　　long tuan xiao nian dou qing chuang

The snowflakes have all fallen in the empty wine jar
Sun on the mountain melts snow that swells the river.
Burner red, cup bright, the lively fire sparkles
Brick tea, little roller of stone, a bushel, bright spot at the
 window.

*

At the window in the sunlit spot, a large roller and small
    brick of tea
Lively fire, a new cup, the shallow burner reddens.
River in flood, the snow melted, sun over the mountains
Jar upside down, wine spent, snowflakes fall in the void.

Bricks of tea were very prized in the period of the Song. Compact, the tea was reduced to powder with the help of a small stone roller before infusing it. A bushel is equivalent to about ten liters, here signifying a large quantity.

Su Dongpo wrote many poems to be sung, especially to the "Pusa man" air that requires alternate lines of seven and five syllables. In two poems entitled "Feeling of Idleness," he arranges the initial and reverse readings by couplets.

Poem 1

閒情	xian qing
火雲凝汗揮珠顆	huo yun ning han hui zhu ke
顆珠揮汗凝雲火	ke zhu hui han ning yun huo
瓊暖碧紗輕	qiong nuan bi sha qing
輕紗碧暖瓊	qing sha bi nuan qiong
暈腮嫌枕印	yun sai xian zhen yin
印枕嫌腮暈	yin zhen xian sai yun
寒照晚妝殘	han zhao wan zhuang can
殘妝晚照寒	can zhuang wan zhao han

Feeling of Idleness

Red clouds of summer make sweat flow, mopping its
    beads
Round beads mopping sweat, red clouds of summer.
Precious softness, the blue screen is light.
Light screen, blue, the smoothness of a precious stone.
Stained cheek on the pillow leaves it print
The pillow bears the mark of the stained cheek.
Cold light, evening make-up softens
Make-up faded, the evening brings cold.

Poem 2

閒情	xian qing
落花閑院春衫薄	luo hua xian yuan chun shan bo
薄衫春院閑花落	bo shan chun yuan xian hua luo
遲日恨依依	chi ri hen yi yi
依依恨日遲	yi yi hen ri chi
夢回鶯舌弄	meng hui ying she nong
弄舌鶯回夢	nong she ying hui meng
郵便問人羞	you bian wen ren xiu
羞人問便郵	xiu ren wen bian you

Feeling of Idleness

Blossoms fallen in the peaceful courtyard, light spring
    dress
Light dress in the spring courtyard, peaceful the blossoms
    fall.
The days lengthen, regrets that cannot be put aside

One cannot stop having regrets, the days go and on.
Returning in dream the oriole who whistles
Whistling the oriole returns in dream.
On the ease of conveying a message, one questions the
　　man with timidity
The timid man asks if it is easy to convey a message.

Two other poems to be sung bear the identical title: "Celebration of Plum Trees." The first is composed to the "Pusa man" air, the second to "The Moon on West River."

嶠南江淺紅梅小　　jiao nan jiang qian hong mei xiao
小梅紅淺江南嶠　　xiao mei hong qian jiang nan jiao
窺我向疏籬　　　　kui wo xiang shu li
籬疏向我窺　　　　li shu xiang wo kui
老人行即到　　　　lao ren xing ji dao
到即行人老　　　　dao ji xing ren lao
離別惜殘枝　　　　li bie xi can zhi
枝殘惜別離　　　　zhi can xi bie li

South of the peak the river is shallow, red plum trees
　　are small
Small red plum trees, the river is shallow at Southern
　　Peak.
To observe it I head toward the thin hedge
The thin hedge stands before me as I look.
An old man approaches, walking
He arrives and draws near, the walker is old.
Separation, regret of the branch that withers
The branch withers deploring separation.

In the following poem, the reverse reading appears in the second part:

馬趁香微路遠	ma chen xiang wei lu yuan
沙籠月淡煙斜	sha long yue dan yan xie
渡波清徹映妍華	du bo qing che ying yan hua
倒綠枝寒鳳掛	dao lü zhi han feng gua
掛鳳寒枝綠倒	gua feng han zhi lü dao
華妍映徹清波渡	hua yan ying che qing bo du
斜煙淡月籠沙	xie yan dan yue long sha
遠路微香趁馬	yuan lu wei xiang chen ma

The horse runs after the fragrances, on the mysterious
    path it grows distant
Sand covers the moon, a pale blanket of mist.
They cross the pure wave, the penetrating reflections
A green branch turned upside down hangs in the cold wind.
Suspended in the wind, leaves on the cold branch turn
    upside down
Beautiful reflections expand, crossing the bright wave.
A blanket of mist veils the moon, covers the sand
On the distant path, a light fragrance follows the horse.

Su Dongpo also wrote a sequence of four quatrains on the four seasons, to be sung to the "Pusa Man" tune:

春	chun
翠環斜慢雲垂耳	cui huan xie man yun chui er
耳垂雲慢斜環翠	er chui yun man xie huan cui
春晚睡昏昏	chun wan shui hun hun

昏昏睡晚春	hun hun shui wan chun
細花黎雪墜	xi hua li xue zhui
墜雪黎花細	zhui xue li hua xi
顰淺念誰人	pin qian nian shui ren
人誰念淺顰	ren shui nian qian pin

Spring

The emerald earring tilts, a soft cloud hangs at the ear
The ear catches the cloud, slowly tilts the emerald earring.
Spring evening, sleep much disturbed
In the darkness falling asleep at the end of spring.
Delicate blossoms, a multitude of flakes fall
Flakes fall, a multitude of delicate blossoms.
With a slight frown, of whom is she thinking?
Of whom thinks this person, frowning slightly?

夏	xia
柳庭風靜人眠晝	liu ting feng jing ren mian zhou
晝眠人靜風庭柳	zhou mian ren jing feng ting liu
香汗薄衫涼	xiang han bo shan liang
涼衫薄汗香	liang shan bo han xiang
手紅冰碗藕	shou hong bing wan ou
藕碗冰紅手	ou wan bing hong shou
郎笑藕絲長	lang xiao ou si chang
長絲藕笑郎	chang si ou xiao lang

Summer

In the courtyard of willows, the wind subsides, someone
    sleeps midday

By day the sleeping person grows quiet, wind in the
    courtyard willows.
Fragrant sweat, the thin dress stays fresh
Cool dress with the light fragrance of sweat.
The hand turns red, an icy bowl of lotus roots
The bowl of lotus roots is icy and turns the hand red.
The man smiles, lotus roots lengthen into threads
The long threads of lotus roots make the man smile.

秋	qiu
井梧雙照新妝冷	jing wu shuang zhao xin zhuang leng
冷妝新照雙梧井	leng zhuang xin zhao shuang wu jing
羞對井花愁	xiu dui jing hua chou
愁花井對羞	chou hua jing dui xiu
影孤憐夜永	ying gu lian ye yong
永夜憐孤影	yong ye lian gu ying
樓上不宜秋	lou shang bu yi qiu
秋宜不上樓	qiu yi bu shang lou

Autumn

The sterculia by the well both gleam with the cold of their
    new finery
The cold finery gleams for a short time on the well by the
    two sterculia.
Troubled before the well, the sad courtesan
    (a flower is a metaphor for courtesan)
The melancholy beauty at the well blushes with shame.
The solitary shadow loves the night that lingers on
The endless night commiserates with the solitary shadow.

High above, the pavilion is not suited to autumn
In autumn it is better not to climb to the pavilion.

| 冬 | dong |

雪花飛暖融香頰　　xue hua fei nuan rong xiang jia
頰香融暖飛花雪　　jia xiang rong nuan fei hua xue
欺雪任單衣　　　　qi xue ren dan yi
衣單任雪欺　　　　yi dan ren xue qi
別時梅子結　　　　bie shi mei zi jie
結子梅時別　　　　jie zi mei shi bie
歸不恨開遲　　　　gui bu hen kai chi
遲開恨不歸　　　　chi kai hen bu gui

Winter

Snowflakes fly and brush kindly against scented cheeks
Scent on the cheeks gently dissipates, snowflakes fly.
Illusion that snow could serve as simple clothing
With simple clothing, resisting the snow is illusory.
At the moment of separation, the plum trees offer their
　　fruits
When the plum trees form their fruits, (comes) the
　　moment of parting.
In returning not regretting their belated blossoming
When they open slowly, regretting not coming back.

Qin Guan (1049–1100)

The great author of *ci*, Qin Guan paid a visit in 1077 to Su Dongpo, who described him as a genius. From then on, the two men remained closely connected. When Su Dongpo fell into disgrace, Qin Guan was not spared. His talent was particularly remarkable in the genre of poems to be sung, but he also wrote prose and regular poems, among them a quatrain and an octet that are reversible.

擬題竇滔妻織錦圖送人   ni ti Dou Tao qi zhi jin tu song ren

悲風鳴葉秋宵涼	bei feng ming ye qiu xiao liang
絲寒縈手淚殘妝	si han ying shou lei can zhuang
微燭窺人愁斷腸	wei zhu kui ren chou duan chang
機翻雲錦妙成章	ji fan yun jin miao cheng zhang

Imitating the Map on a Woven Brocade by the Wife of Dou Tao, Offered to a Friend

Sad wind whistles in the leaves, night of autumn cold
Silk threads are wound trembling around the hand, tears
    spoil make-up.
Watching by the weak glow of a candle, this person's
    melancholy breaks the heart
On the loom, turning, returning, the marvelous brocade
    composes a text.

*

The text composes a marvelous brocade, clouds upside
down on the loom
Heart broken by a melancholy person, she watches the
candle that grows dim.
Make-up ruined by tears, the hand winds silk threads
trembling with cold
Icy night, autumn leaves rustle sadly in the wind.

即席次君禮年兄韻   ji xi ci jun li nian xiong yun

情舒喜面山浮翠	qing shu xi mian shan fu cui
袖滿薰風涼透時	xiu man xun feng liang tou shi
萍碎錦鱗金網舉	ping sui jin lin jin wang ju
影差簾燕玉鉤垂	ying cha lian yan yu gou chui
輕輕篆鼎凝香細	qing qing zhuan ding ning xiang xi
款款方壺轉漏遲	kuan kuan fang hu zhuan lou chi
清興此來同約久	qing xing ci lai tong yue jiu
越多深意古人詩	yue duo shen yi gu ren shi

During a Banquet, on the Rhymes of the Master, Offered to a Dear Friend

Feelings spread over the joyful face, mountains drift, blue-
green
Sleeves fill with warm wind (from the brazier), when the
chill penetrates.
Duckweed disperses, scales in bright colors, the golden
net reemerges
The shadow grows distant, swallow at the blind, jade hook
hangs.

Lightly the carved perfume burner concentrates the
    incense's delicacy
Slowly the square vase reflects the water clock's delay.
Subtle pleasure coming together thus bound forever
Making known deep thoughts, poems of ancient authors.

*

Ancient thoughts of poets, many are expressed with depth
Long bound, meeting again, this pleasure remains pure.
The water clock that slows topples the vase, is adjusted
    slowly
Delicate incense is concentrated in the perfume burner,
    seals lightly engraved.
Hook suspended, the jade swallow, the blind distances its
    shadow
Net reemerging, golden scales, bright colors disperse the
    duckweed.
Sometimes cool wind penetrates, steam (from the brazier)
    fills sleeves
A bluish (mist) envelopes the mountains, joy in expressing
    one's feelings.

Yuwen Xuzhong (1079–1146)

Originally from Chengdu in present-day Sichuan, Yuwen Xuzhong first served the Southern Song rulers. Sent by Emperor Gaozong on assignment with the Jin, he was taken prisoner. Once freed, he switched sides and took up the post of secretary of the Ministry of Rites. Although he enjoyed a certain prestige, he was nonetheless accused of plotting a conspiracy. Following his conviction, he was once again thrown into prison and then assassinated without having been sentenced. This turbulent historical context marked his work, yet he seems close to a certain *chan* (zen) spirit. Among the fifty poems attributed to him, we find a beautiful sequence of twelve reversible poems on the four seasons.

Spring 1

短草鋪茸綠	duan cao pu rong lü
殘梅照雪稀	can mei zhao xue xi
暖輕還錦褥	nuan qing huan jin ru
寒峭怯羅衣	han qiao qie luo yi

The short grass expands, verdant
The withered plum tree is reflected in sparse snow.
Warmly dressed, returning light-hearted to the rich
    dwelling
The harsh cold makes fearful light clothes.

*

Light clothes make fearful the harsh cold
With riches and honors, returning luxuriously dressed.
Scattered snow shines on the withered plum tree
Verdant, the short grass expands.

Spring 2

翠漣冰綻日	cui lian bing zhan ri
香徑晚多花	xiang jing wan duo hua
細筍抽蒲密	xi sun chou pu mi
長條舞柳斜	chang tiao wu liu xie

Blue as far as the eye can see, ice melts under the sun
Fragrant path, evening, many blossoms.
Young lanky shoots, rushes emerge, thick
Long willow branches that sway.

*

Bent willows, long branches dance
Dense rushes, young shoots emerge, delicate.
Blossoms are numerous, evening, the path scented
Sun pierces the uniformly bluish ice.

Spring 3

折花幽檻小	zhe hua you jian xiao
傾酒綠杯深	qing jiu lü bei shen
蝶舞輕風曉	die wu qing feng xiao
鶯啼老樹陰	ying ti lao shu yin

Gathering blossoms at the little buried gate
Pouring wine in the deep, green cup.
A butterfly dances in the light dawn wind
An oriole sings in the shade of the old tree.

*

In the shady tree, an old oriole sings
In the dawn wind, a light butterfly dances.
In the deep cup, the green wine is poured
At the little gate, gathering buried blossoms.

Summer 1

翠密團窗竹	cui mi tuan chuang zhu
青圓貼水荷	qing yuan tie shui he
睡多嫌晝永	shui duo xian zhou yong
醒少得風和	xing shao de feng he

Bluish and thick, bamboo gather at the window
Green and round, lotus cling to the water.
Those who sleep much complain that the days go on and on.
Those who rarely emerge from drunkenness are glad that
    the wind is soft.

*

Soft wind, happy to be half awake
Endless day, displeased to sleep much.
Lotus and water cling to each other in the perfection of
    their green
Window and bamboo unite in the thickness of their blue.

Summer 2

草徑迷深綠	cao jing mi shen lü
蓮池浴膩紅	lian chi yu ni hong
早蟬鳴樹曲	zao chan ming shu qu
鮮鯉躍潭東	xian li yue tan dong

Path in the grass, wandering in deep greenery
Lotus pond, washing red from the mud.
Morning cicadas sing in the hollows of the trees
Lively carp leap east of the ornamental lake.

*

In the eastern ornamental lake, carp leap with vigor
In gnarled trees, cicadas sing early morning.
Of the red mud, pond lotus are washed
Deep green, grasses hide the path.

Summer 3

暴雨隨雲驟	bao yu sui yun zhou
驚雷隱地平	jing lei yin di ping
好風搖箑透	hao feng yao sha tou
輕汗挹冰清	qing han yi bing qing

Torrential rain follows the clouds that pass
Frightful lightning disappears on the horizon.
A refreshing breeze from the fan that waves
A light sweat borrows its transparency from ice.

*

Transparent ice, sweat beads lightly
The penetrating fan raises a refreshing breeze.
The plain absorbs the ringing of thunder
Clouds that pass follow the bursts of rain.

Autumn 1

晚日欣簾捲	wan ri xin lian juan
涼風覺袂搖	liang feng jue mei yao
遠吟高興遣	yuan yin gao xing qian
長醉宿愁銷	chang zui su chou xiao

At sunset, glad to raise the blind
Cool wind is felt in sleeves that stir.
In a distant song, great exhilaration dissipates
In deep drunkenness, an old melancholy fades.

*

Melancholy vanished, passing the night in great
    drunkeness
Exhilaration dissipated, a powerful song grows distant.
Fluttering sleeves reveal the coolness of the wind
Blinds rolled up, admiring the sunset.

Autumn 2

短葦低殘雨	duan wei di can yu
虛舟帶晚潮	xu zhou dai wan chao
斷鴻歸暗浦	duan hong gui an pu
疏葉墮寒梢	shu ye duo han shao

Short reeds flattened by rain
Empty boat borne by the evening tide.
Wild geese separated, return to the dark bank
Scattered leaves fall from cold branches.

*

Ends of the branches frozen, fallen leaves scatter
The bank is dark, geese returned separately.
Evening tide brings an empty boat
Rain ruins the flattened reeds.

Autumn 3

慼慼蛬吟苦	qi qi qiong yin ku
茫茫水驛孤	mang mang shui yi gu
日銜山色暮	ri xian shan se mu
霜帶菊叢枯	shuang dai ju cong ku

Sad, sad, the cricket sings its sorrow
Vast, vast, the waters of the isolated postal way.
Sun takes on the colors of the mountain in setting
Frost makes wither the chrysanthemum groves.

*

Groves withered, chrysanthemums covered with frost
Colors of sunset, the mountain beside the sun.
Isolated station, the water vast, vast
Singing with difficulty, a cricket, sad, sad.

Winter 1

鶻健呼風急	hu jian hu feng ji
鳥啼促景殘	niao ti cu jing can
窟深宜兔蟄	ku shen yi tu zhe
蒲折蔭魚寒	pu zhe yin yu han

Tireless vultures cry, the wind is strong
Birds hasten to sing, the light declines.
The deep hole suits the hare who curls up there
Bent rushes protect the fish from cold.

*

Numb fish protect themselves in the bent rushes
The sluggish hare makes do with a deep hole.
The declining light urges birds to sing
Strong winds roar over hardy vultures.

Winter 2

裂瓦寒霜重	lie wa han shuang zhong
鋪窗月影清	pu chuang yue ying qing
滅燈驚好夢	mie deng jing hao meng
孤枕念深情	gu zhen nian shen qing

On cracked tiles, cold frost weighs heavy
Spread across the window, distinct shadow of the moon.
The lamp going out disturbs a pleasant dream
On the lonely pillow, thinking of one's deep feelings.

*

Deep feelings, thinking of them on the lonely pillow
Pleasant dream, disturbed by the lamp going out.
Distinct shadow, the moon at the window spreads
Heavy frost, the cold tiles crack.

Winter 3

秀柏留陰綠	xiu bai liu yin lü
芳梅蘸影斜	fang mei zhan ying xie
留簷冰結玉	liu yan bing jie yu
裝樹雪飛花	zhuang shu xue fei hua

Slender cypress retain green shade
Fragrant plum trees are submerged in low shadow.
At the edge of the roof, ice catches in jade
Decorating the trees, snowflakes fly.

*

Blossoms fly, snow adorns trees
Jade catches in ice at the edge of the roof.
Low shadow covers fragrant plum trees
Green shade remains, slender cypress.

Yang Wanli (1127–1206)

Without ever including the highest administrative offices, except perhaps that of director of the Imperial Library, Yang Wanli's career as government official went through the usual vicissitudes: exiles followed by reinstatements and vice versa. In the end, he rejected all positions to live as a hermit and devote himself to the practice of *chan* (zen). Among his many poems appears a regular quatrain that can be read reversibly.

富陽登舟待潮回文 fu yang deng zhou dai chao hui wen

山按江清江按天	shan an jiang qing jiang an tian
老人漁釣下前灘	lao ren yu diao xia qian tan
寒潮晚到風無定	han chao wan dao feng wu ding
船泊小灣春日殘	chuan bo xiao wan chun ri can

Boarding a Boat in Fuyang to Await the Tide

The mountain looks to the clarity of the river, the river
    looks to the sky
An old man goes angling, descends to the near bank.
Cold tide, evening arrives, the wind turns
The boat drops anchor in the small cove, the spring
    sun sets.

*

Sun setting in the spring cove, a small boat anchored
Peacefully, without wind, evening tide arrives, cold.
In front of the bank descends the hook of the old
    fisherman
Sky looks to the clarity of the river, the river looks to the
    mountain.

Zhu Xi (1130–1200)

This great thinker, philosopher, and scholar wrote commentaries on the major works of the Confucian school, the *I Ching*, and the *Book of Songs*. His interpretations dominated Chinese thought until the end of the empire. Zhu Xi left a significant body of work, including more than one hundred volumes of prose and a few volumes of poetry and two reversible poems to be sung:

菩薩蠻──次圭甫韻　　Pusa man ci gui fu yun

暮江寒碧縈長路	mu jiang han bi ying chang lu
路長縈碧寒江暮	lu chang ying bi han jiang mu
花塢夕陽斜	hua wu xi yang xie
斜陽夕塢花	xie yang xi wu hua
客愁無勝集	ke chou wu sheng ji
集勝無愁客	ji sheng wu chou ke
醒似醉多情	xing si zui duo qing
情多醉似醒	qing duo zui si xing

To the Pusa Man Tune, on the Rhymes of Master Gui

At sunset the cold river is blue-green, it winds around the
　　long path
The path winds at length around the green river cold at
　　sunset.
On the flowered rampart, oblique rays of twilight

Oblique rays of twilight on the rampart flowers.
Worries of the traveler with no end in sight accumulate
Reaping the victory, traveler without a care.
Awakening like drunkenness because of many feelings
Through many feelings, drunkenness resembles awakening.

菩薩蠻──呈秀野   Pusa man cheng xiu ye

晚紅飛盡春寒淺	wan hong fei jin chun han qian
淺寒春盡飛紅晚	qian han chun jin fei hong wan
尊酒綠陰繁	zun jiu lü yin fan
繁陰綠酒尊	fan yin lü jiu zun
老仙詩句好	lao xian shi ju hao
好句詩仙老	hao ju shi xian lao
長恨送年芳	chang hen song nian fang
芳年送恨長	fang nian song hen chang

To the Pusa Man Tune, the Flowering Country of Cheng

The glow of evening softens, the spring chill is light
Light chill, spring draws to a close, drifting glow of
    evening.
Cups of green wine, shadows are many
Many green shadows of wine cups.
From the old immortal the poetic lines are beautiful
Poems in beautiful lines, the immortal is old.
He long regrets the scents that accompany the years
The fragrant years bring longtime regrets. (The fragrant
    years are those of youth)

MING DYNASTY
(1368–1644)

For almost ninety years, a foreign dynasty of Mongol origin ruled China: the Yuan dynasty. When the Ming dynasty succeeded it, a return to the foundations of *han* culture occurred in the Chinese empire, with renewed interest in Confucianism and the great classics in general. For its part, literary criticism applied its efforts to generic classification, establishing a rigorous demarcation between orthodox forms (*zhengti*) and altered forms (*bianti*). Reversible poems were definitively relegated to that second category. The idea that they were only literary diversions probably dates from this period. Moreover, poetry was not the primary preoccupation of Ming writers, whose innovations involved the novel. But the memory of Su Hui being ever vivid, a few authors took an interest in the reversible poem nonetheless, and contributed to the perpetuation of the genre.

Qiu Jun (1418/1421–1495)

A government official who served most notably as secretary of the Office of Rites, Qui Jun enjoyed something of a reputation in his lifetime. Today he is considered a minor author because of his adherence to "feudal morality"! Essentially a playwright, he left us two reversible poems: a heptasyllabic octet and a poem to be sung.

夜宿江館	ye su jiang guan
潮生海岸兩崖傾	chao sheng hai an liang ya qing
落月江楓映火明	luo yue jiang feng ying huo ming
橋透白波流水遠	qiao tou bai bo liu shui yuan
屋連紅樹帶霜清	wu lian hong shu dai shuang qing
迢迢漏盡寒更曉	tiao tiao lou jin han geng xiao
片片雲妝夜雨晴	pian pian yun zhuang ye yu qing
遙望楚天江渺渺	yao wang chu tian jiang miao miao
茭蒲盡處落鴻輕	jiao pu jin chu luo hong qing

Passing the Night at the River Inn

Tide gives shape to the seashore, two sloping banks
Setting moon, river maples, fire is reflected sparkling.
The bridge penetrates white waves, water flows growing
    distant
The house brushes against red trees, a pure frost covers
    them.

Drop by drop the water clock empties, cold hours of
dawn
One by one the clouds turn color, sun breaks through
after night rain.
Viewing far off the Chu sky, the river as far as the eye
can see
In spots covered with water grass and bulrushes, wild
geese land lightly.

*

The place where wild geese land is covered with bulrushes
and water grass.
Vast, vast, the sky above the river, gazing toward Chu in
the distance.
Sunny spell and rain, night finery the clouds in strata
Just before dawn the cold is at its height, the water clock
drop by drop.
Trees covered with pure frost, red the adjoining houses
Waves dispersing from distant waters, bridge penetrating
the foam.
Sparkling fire is reflected in maples, moon on the river sets
Steep sides of two banks, the sea gives rise to the tide.

The second text is a poem to be sung "to the tune of Pusa
man." Thus it has the same prosodic structure as the poems by Su
Dongpo presented above. Nevertheless Qiu Jun does not arrange
for the reversal of the lines in the poem. The reverse reading takes
place line by line, following the same order, that is, beginning with
the two seven-syllable lines.

秋思　　　　　　　　　qiu si

紗窗碧透橫斜影　　　sha chuang bi tou heng xie ying
月光寒處空幃冷　　　yue guang han chu kong wei leng
香炷細燒檀　　　　　xiang zhu xi shao tan
沉沉正夜閔　　　　　chen chen zheng ye min
更深方閑睡　　　　　geng shen fang xian shui
倦極生愁思　　　　　juan ji sheng chou si
含情感寂廖　　　　　han qing gan ji liao
何處別魂銷　　　　　he chu bie hun xiao

Autumn Thoughts

Window screen penetrated by the blue of a transverse
　　shadow
In moonlight, frozen place, cold curtain in the emptiness.
Scented candle, the sandalwood is delicately consumed
Heavy, heavy, the sufferings in the depth of night.
Deeper still, the sleep of idleness
An extreme weariness breeds sad thoughts.
Suppressed feelings prompt silence and grief
To what place do souls separated from bodies disappear?

*

The shadow penetrates slantwise the bluish window screen
A cold curtain in an empty place, icy light of the moon.
Sandalwood burns, the thin candle is fragrant
Night of suffering, heavy, heavy.
Sleeping in idleness, it is even deeper
The sadness of thoughts engender extreme fatigue.
Grief and silence, feelings experienced are buried
The place where vanished souls have gone, where is it?

Wang Shizhen (1526–1590)

Descending from an old family of literati, Wang Shizhen left a profuse and voluminous body of work, featuring these two poems to be sung:

菩薩蠻──春暮	Pusa man chun mu
白楊長映孤山碧	bai yang chang ying gu shan bi
碧山孤映長楊白	bi shan gu ying chang yang bai
春暮別傷人	chun mu bie shang ren
人傷別暮春	ren shang bie mu chun
雁歸迷塞遠	yan gui mi sai yuan
遠塞迷歸雁	yuan sai mi gui yan
樓倚獨深愁	lou yi du shen chou
愁深獨倚樓	chou shen du yi lou

To the Pusa Man Tune, Spring Twilight

White poplars with lengthened reflections, Solitary
    Mountain emerald green
The emerald mountain is reflected alone, the tall poplars
    are white.
In spring twilight, separation grieves a being
Person wounded by separation, twilight spring.
Wild geese return wandering to the distance of the
    marches

The distant marches lead returning wild geese astray.
Leaning against the pavilion, alone, deep melancholy
Melancholy is deep, leaning alone at the pavilion.

菩薩蠻──閨思   **Pusa man gui si**

斷風依約愁砧亂	duan feng yi yue chou zhen luan
亂砧愁約依風斷	luan zhen chou yue yi feng duan
無語對燈孤	wu yu dui deng gu
孤燈對語無	gu deng dui yu wu
冷香留去影	leng xiang liu qu ying
影去留香冷	ying qu liu xiang leng
思後夢來期	si hou meng lai qi
期來夢後思	qi lai meng hou si

To the Pusa Man Tune, Thoughts in the Gynoecium

Bitter wind like worries beats confusedly
The confused beating of worry ceases with the wind.
Without a word facing the solitude of the lamp
Solitary lamp facing silence.
Cold scents retain the vanished shadow
The shadow is gone leaving a fragrant chill.
After meditating comes the moment of the dream
The moment comes after the dream, thinking of it.

Tang Xianzu (1550–1616)

Tang Xianzu is the most famous playwright of the Ming dynasty. His masterpiece, "The Peony Pavilion" is one of the most widely performed stock plays. The story of love it recounts is as famous in China as "Romeo and Juliet" is in the West. Before being banished by the emperor, Tang also held the position of secretary of the Office of Rites. He was undoubtedly moved by the story of Su Hui, as demonstrated by two reversible poems to be sung "to the tune of Pusa man," one of which appears here.

擬織婦閨怨	ni zhi fu gui yuan
梅題遠色春歸得	mei ti yuan se chun gui de
遲鄉瘴嶺過愁各	chi xiang zhang ling guo chou ge
孤影雁回斜	gu ying yan hui xie
峰寒逼翠紗	feng han bi cui sha
窗殘拋錦室	chuang can pao jin shi
織急還催織	zhi ji hai cui zhi
錦官當夕情	jin guan dang xi qing
啼斷望河明	ti duan wang he ming

In Imitation of the Gynoecium Complaints of the Weaver

Plum trees display their color in the distance, spring is
    returning
Making his way slowly toward the homeland, crossing
    mountain chains in muggy air, the sad traveler.

Solitary shadow cast by a goose who returns
Cold summit resembling blue-green silk.
Broken window, flinging the shuttle in the brocade
    workshop
Weaving in haste, getting busy again weaving.
The brocade is in keeping with twilight feelings
Tears cease, contemplating the Milky Way that shines.

*

Rediscovering the colors of spring, plum trees on display
    in the distance
The traveler is sad crossing the mountain chains, muggy
    air of the homeland, he walks slowly.
Returning, diagonal, the solitary shadow of the goose
Blue-green silk near the cold peak.
In the room, a brocade, turning away from the broken
    window
Weaving anxiously, once again hurrying to weave.
Twilight feelings are in keeping with the brocade
Contemplating the shining Milky Way interrupts tears.

Beyond the allusion to Su Hui, the poet also evokes the legend of the "Herdsman and the Weaver," two stars separated by the Milky Way that can only meet once a year on the seventh day of the seventh month, when magpies form a bridge that allows the Herdsman to rejoin the Weaver. The sixth line, in reverse, recalls the "to walk to walk again to walk to walk" of the "Nineteen Ancient Poems" with its "weaving/hastening/once again/hurrying/weaving."

Li Yang (?)

Unfortunately, there is no information available to us on this author, who left a sequence of about eighty heptasyllabic reversible poems, under the general title of *Celebration of Spring*. Each poem also has its own title, in two characters of which the first is invariably the word "spring": "Spring Snow," "Spring Wind," Spring Clouds," "Spring Moon," "Spring Dew," "Spring Rain," "Spring Mist," "Spring Forest," "Spring Temple," "Spring Separation." I have extracted five of them:

Poem 1

春雪	chun xue
遙山四起暮雲同	yao shan si qi mu yun tong
素積庭階半卷風	su ji ting jie ban juan feng
橋外柳花飛點點	qiao wai liu hua fei dian dian
烏邊梅影淡蒙蒙	wu bian mei ying dan meng meng
飆回舞徑春馴鶴	biao hui wu jing chun xun he
絮落沾泥曉踏鴻	xu luo zhan ni xiao ta hong
廖寂苦吟人耐冷	liao ji ku yin ren nai leng
遙誰共醉小亭東	yao shui gong zui xiao ting dong

Spring Snow

The surrounding distant mountains rise up like clouds at sunset
Whiteness amassed in the courtyard staircase, half raised
    by the wind.

Beyond the bridge, willow blossoms fly in all directions
Beside the rampart, the shadow of plum trees, light, light.
A whirlwind returns, dancing on the springtime path, the
    familiar cranes
Down falls, soiled by the mud, at dawn wild geese trample it.
Alone and melancholy, singing sadly, the man endures the
    cold
Who to invite to get drunk together east of the small
    pavilion?

*

In the eastern pavilion, slightly drunk, with whom to
    make the most of it?
In the cold, the hardy man sings to himself, he suffers
    melancholic and alone.
Wild geese trample the mud at dawn, down falls, wet
Cranes return one after another on the springtime path,
    dancing whirlwind.
Fine, fine, the pale shadow, beside plum trees a rampart
In all directions fly blossoms, willow beyond the bridge.
Wind whirls halfway up the stairs, in the courtyard white
    accumulates
Similar clouds rise at sunset, everywhere in the distance,
    mountains.

Poem 18

春園   **chun yuan**

家園灌引水西東   jia yuan guan yin shui xi dong
繚繞溪煙帶霧籠   liao rao xi yan dai wu long

鴉噪樹頭山聳翠　　ya zao shu tou shan song cui
蝶飛籬腳日流紅　　die fei li jiao ri liu hong
花叢一簇方情麗　　hua cong yi cu fang qing li
草徑三開幻色空　　cao jing san kai huan se kong
遮莫雪梅殘點點　　zhe mo xue mei can dian dian
花年惜去賞心同　　hua nian xi qu shang xin tong

Spring Garden

The family garden irrigated by water from west to east
Mist from the waterfall covers it in curls.
Crows cawing at the height of the trees, mountains rise
　　up bluish
Butterflies fly at the base of the hedge, the sun shoots its
　　red rays.
Groves in blossom form one mass, the scent of spring is
　　pleasant
The grassy path divides in three, unreal colors changing.
No matter that plum trees are wilting under snow
The good years regretfully pass, the happy heart is always
　　the same.

*

Similar hearts take delight, tight-fisted with time
Plum trees gradually wilt, snow does not cover them.
Giving the illusion of opening onto sky, three paths of grass
Beautiful fragrant mass, a grove of blossoms.
Red rays of the sun, in the hedge fly butterflies
Bluish summits of looming mountains, in the trees caw crows.
Bearing a layer of mist, the winding waterfall
Water runs from east to west, irrigating garden and house.

Poem 19

春水   chun shui

喃喃語燕舞回汀	nan nan yu yan wu hui ting
望入長天極渺冥	wang ru chang tian ji miao ming
帆颭晚煙溪繞碧	fan zhan wan yan xi rao bi
鷺拳寒雨浦浮青	lu quan han yu pu fu qing
衫松洋影清波疊	shan song yang ying qing bo die
藻荇留香細浪清	zao xing liu xiang xi lang qing
岩削石棱春映水	yan xiao shi leng chun ying shui
嵌空半蠢遠山屏	qian kong ban chu yuan shan ping

Spring Waters

"Nan nan," the swallows scatter flying toward shore
They hope to penetrate the most inaccessible heights of
    sky.
A sail bobbing in evening mist, serpent river, bluish
Egrets huddle in cold rain, river banks drift, green.
Shadow stirred by cypress and pine, transparent waves
    follow one another
Persistent scent of algae and duckweed, wave delicate and
    pure.
Peaks divide rocks into jutting angles, in spring they are
    reflected in the water
It rises up partly inlaid in the sky, in the distance the
    mountainous shelter.

*

Folded mountains rise in the distance, half inlaid in
    the sky

Water in spring reflects overhanging rocks, jagged peaks.
A pure wave delicately scented is retained by duckweed
    and algae
Successive waves of transparent shadow, they stir pine and
    cypress.
River banks drift in the green, the cold rain on huddling
    egrets
Serpent river bluish, evening mist, a bobbing sail.
Inaccessible heights of the sky where the gaze long
    penetrates
Returning toward shore swallows wheel, crying
    "nan nan."

Poem 28

春寺   chun si

松澗幽攀客罷吟	song jian you pan ke ba yin
閉關禪定淡機心	bi guan chan ding dan ji xin
鐘聞夜靜初驚夢	zhong wen ye jing chu jing meng
梵響晴空遠度音	fan xiang qing kong yuan du yin
濃露滴花黃滿徑	nong lu di hua huang man jing
細風吹竹翠饒林	xi feng chui zhu cui rao lin
峰高上處閑隨喜	feng gao shang chu xian sui xi
胸蕩雲天橫碧岑	xiong dang yun tian heng bi cen

Spring Monastery

Climbing in a solitary place of pines and streams, the
    traveler stops to sing
Isolated and contemplative in meditation, the mind
    without artifice.

Bell perceived in the night calm, pulled abruptly from
> dream
Sacred texts resonate in the calm emptiness, their sound
> spreads far.
Abundant dew collects on flowers, yellow they cover the
> path
Light wind blows in bamboo, emerald they fill the forest.
At the highest point of the summit, delighting completely
> at ease
The soul is purified in the cloudy sky, crosswise bluish peaks.

*

Bluish peaks across the sky, clouds purify the soul
Conforming with joy to this peaceful place, climbing the
> high summit.
In thick forest, emerald bamboo, wind blows lightly
The path is covered with yellow flowers, dew in abundant
> drops.
A sound crosses this vast space, in the sunlit spot sacred
> texts resonate
Surprising dream at first so peaceful, night, hearing the bell.
Tricks of the mind weaken in concentration, isolation and
> contemplation of meditation
The song breaks off when the traveler climbs among
> streams and lonely pines.

Many expressions belonging to the Buddhist vocabulary ap-
pear in this poem. Some are polysemous, such as *sui xi* in the
next-to-last line, which can mean either to do what one wants,
completely free, following one's personal inclination, or to go visit

temples and pagodas. The last half of line seven can also mean to peacefully visit temples and pagodas.

Poem 74

春夜　　　　　　　chun ye

缸紅照夜半開軒	gang hong zhao ye ban kai xuan
是處聞聲萬籟喧	shi chu wen sheng wan lai xuan
尨吠聚虜茅舍密	mang fei ju lu mao she mi
鶴馴幽徑竹隱繁	he xun you jing zhu yin fan
腔新制曲歌明月	qiang xin zhi qu ge ming yue
漏疊催籌舉綠樽	lou die cui chou ju lü zun
雙眼醉迷花弄影	shuang yan zui mi hua nong ying
紗窗碧鎖淡煙村	sha chuang bi suo dan yan cun

Spring Night

The red jar gleams in the night, window half-open
From this spot one hears the sound of ten thousand
　　echoing cries.
Dogs bark in village houses, my thatch hut is peaceful
Cranes arrive gradually along the dark path, the shadow
　　of bamboo is thick.
Composing a piece to a new tune, extolling the light of
　　the moon
The water clock ceaselessly hurries along, raising a cup of
　　wine.
A pair of eyes lost in drunkenness, blossoms play at hiding
Bluish screen at the window, village in pale mist.

*

Pale screen of mist over the village, bluish mosquito net at
    the window
Shadow makes blossoms illusory, a pair of drunken eyes.
Counting the raised cups of wine, hurrying uninterrupted
    sound of the water clock
Song of the moonlit brightness offers a new tune.
Many shadows in the bamboo path, cranes gradually
    arrive in the darkness
In houses and thatch huts, dogs gather and bark.
Ten thousand sounds of echoing clamor, from this spot
    one hears them
Window open in the middle of the night, illuminated by
    the oil lamp.

In the first line, *gang* means "jar," and *hong* means "red": the red jar. In the reverse reading, *honggang* means "oil lamp." In the third line the word *mao* (reed), is combined with different words, *maoshe* or *maolu* to designate a thatch hut in both cases.

Cao Fengzu (?)

Without information on dates, we cannot know if Cao Fengzu was a contemporary of Li Yang, if the two poets knew one another, or if one of them knew the other's work. Still, the eighty reversible poems, *On the Women's Quarters, Flowers, and the Moon*, are oddly reminiscent of the preceding collection. Cao nevertheless added his own personal touch. The sequence is divided into sixty-four heptasyllabic octets and sixteen heptasyllabic quatrains based on the titles of those sixty-four octets. Here are the first four octets followed by the quatrain created from their titles.

Poem 1

春吟獨酌小窗幽　　chun yin du zhuo xiao chuang you

華春惜物詠詩工　　hua chun xi wu yong shi gong
韻步閑韻小閣東　　yun bu xian yun xiao ge dong
茶煮夜煙沉院竹　　cha zhu ye yan chen yuan zhu
硯飄時雨過窗桐　　yan piao shi yu guo chuang tong
花生粉面三分白　　hua sheng fen mian san fen bai
酒濕朱唇一點紅　　jiu shi zhu chun yi dian hong
嘩隔遠塵香踏玉　　hua ge yuan chen xiang ta yu
紗廚透影碎簾風　　sha chu tou ying sui lian feng

In Spring Singing and Drinking Alone at the
Little Remote Window

Bright spring, attached to natural beings, devoting oneself
  to poetry
With borrowed rhymes, composing peacefully east of the
  small pavilion.
Tea steeps, nocturnal mist, bamboo in the inner courtyard
A timely rain falls on the ink stone by the sterculia at the
  window.
A blossom appears on the powdered face, three dabs of
  white
Moist wine on a vermilion lip, one spot of red.
Clamor distances the faraway world, a walk fragrant with
  spring
Shadow crosses the gauze screen, blind broken by wind.

*

Shadow broken by the partition crosses the gauze of the
  screen
You walk on the fragrant dust, long distant the clamor.
Red punctuates a vermilion lip moist with wine
White divides the face into three, make-up resembles a
  blossom.
The sterculia window lets in the rain, it sometimes falls on
  the ink stone
In the bamboo courtyard, heavy mist, night tea steeps.
In East Pavilion, a mistaken rhyme, walking idly while
  composing
The ingenious poem celebrates natural beings, attached to
  the brightness of spring.

Poem 2

影對寒燈一結愁	ying dui han deng yi jie chou
卿居別院小西湖	qing ju bie yuan xiao xi hu
薄命人悲自向隅	bo ming ren bei zi xiang yu
清影妾知方照燭	qing ying qie zhi fang zhao zhu
暖心郎比那熏鑪	nuan xin lang bi na xun lu
名成為恨留花譜	ming cheng wei hen liu hua pu
面對如看入畫圖	mian dui ru kan ru hua tu
更盡夜含雙眼淚	geng jin ye han shuang yan lei
情深感泣複還珠	qing shen gan qi fu huan zhu

In the Dark, Facing the Lone Lamp,
Melancholy Suddenly Arises

You live in another residence on small West Lake
The man saddened by his unhappy fate is desolate in a
    corner.
The wife with transparent shadow knows this, while
    the candle glows
The husband with gentle heart resembles this incense
    burner.
His name like a regret is retained in the flower album
His face as though looking at me is in the painting.
Night watch ends, the night contained tears from my
    two eyes
Feelings arouse tears, once again come their pearls.

*

Like pearls come tears again, feelings deeply shattering
Eyes in tears, the couple contain (their feelings), night

ends with the watch (a division of time into watches
of two hours each).

The painting penetrates the gaze like a face face-to-face

Flowers in the album retain the regret of being well
named.

The incense burner is comparable to the gentleness of the
man's heart

When the candle glows, one knows the shadow of the
light woman.

In a corner, turned toward his sadness, the man's fate is
indifferent

In the small residence west of the lake, the beloved lives
apart.

"Flowers in the album retain the regret of being well named" is
an allusion to concubines in the women's quarters who aspire to
worthiness while awaiting a title.

Poem 3

鄰女情妝停繡彩　　lin nü qian zhuang ting xiu cai

東鄰女過晚慵妝	dong lin nü guo wan yong zhuang
繡罷仍拈恨線長	xiu ba reng nian hen xian chang
絨睡碎霞春茜色	rong shui sui xia chun qian se
鏡開新月夜涵光	jing kai xin yue ye han guang
紅顏玉盞三分酒	hong yan yu zhan san fen jiu
紫鈿金壚一燭香	zi dian jin lu yi zhu xiang
風信惜花看去倦	feng xin xi hua kan qu juan
桐窗倚竹醉吟芳	tong chuang yi zhu zui yin fang

The Young Neighbor Girl with Elegant Finery
Interrupts her Multicolored Embroidery

The young neighbor girl from the east passes, evening,
    with her side bun
Embroidery halted, she winds the thread once again,
    regretting that it lengthens.
A blanket for lying down, light springtime clouds, color of
    madder
Open mirror, the new moon floods the night with its
    light.
Color of red, in a jade cup three measures of wine
Crimson inlay on the gilded perfume burner, a stick of
    incense.
In the seasonal wind, blossoms seem to get tired
Sterculia window, leaning on bamboo, drunk, singing of
    its fragrance.

*

Singing prettily of drunkenness, bamboo leaning on the
    sterculia by the window
Tired from going to see blossoms, regretting the seasonal
    wind.
Incense stick as soon as it burns, gold is inlaid with
    crimson
Wine shared in three cups, jade tinged with red.
The moon sheds its light in the night, mirror newly open
Madder colored clouds of spring, a light blanket for
    sleeping.
Long thread twisted with regret, once again halting her
    embroidery

Hair in a bun, evening, the young neighbor girl passes
    heading east.

In the first line, the neighbor girl from the east is an allusion to
a poem by Song Yu (third century BCE), signifying a beautiful
woman.

Poem 4

管弦新學見人羞   guan xian xin xue jian ren xiu

湮湮夜雨灑簾旌   yan yan ye yu sa lian jing
袖嫋餘香豔惜聲   xiu niao yu xiang yan xi sheng
唇動暗歌時曲細   chun dong an ge shi qu xi
眼抬偷見晚妝輕   yan tai tou jian wan zhuang qing
神情寓意深調瑟   shen qing yu yi shen tiao se
語笑迎歡乍弄笙   yu xiao ying huan zha nong sheng
新試巧音嬌澀指   xin shi qiao yin jiao se zhi
人憐弱柳暮啼鶯   ren lian ruo liu mu ti ying

Flute and Lute Recently Learned, She Sees Someone and Blushes with Shame

With big drops nocturnal rain splashes the curtain of the
    door
A heady perfume rises from sleeves, the beautiful woman
    loves music.
Her lips move, for an imperceptible song sometimes the
    tune is refined
She lifts her eyes, steals a look, evening finery is light.
Mind and feelings suggest their intentions, zither with
    intense melody

Words and laughter announce pleasure, mouth pipes'
    unexpected sound.
New attempt at seductive tones, fingers frail or tough
The man cherishes the flexible willow, at sunset orioles sing.

*

Orioles sing at sunset in the willows, weak they inspire
    people's pity
Displaying tones hard or delicate, attempting cleverness
    with novelty.
Sound of the mouth pipes, suddenly rapid, prompts
    laughter and talk
Melody of the zither, with deep meaning, reflects feelings
    and mind.
Lightly made-up, seeing the evening, lifting the gaze to the
    hidden
Refined tune, the song of the moment, lips move
    imperceptibly.
Renowned beauty, her heady perfume rises in her sleeves
Sign and curtain are splashed by rain, night plunged into
    water.

The flexible willow in the first reading is nothing other than the
thin waist of a pretty woman.

Quatrain 1, composed of the titles of the four preceding
poems:

春吟獨酌小窗幽	chun yin du zhuo xiao chuang you
影對寒燈一結愁	ying dui han deng yi jie chou
鄰女倩妝停繡彩	lin nü qian zhuang ting xiu cai
管弦新學見人羞	guan xian xin xue jian ren xiu

In spring singing and drinking alone at the little remote
window
In the dark, facing the lone lamp, melancholy suddenly
arises.
The young neighbor girl with elegant finery interrupts
her embroidery
Flute and lute recently learned, she sees someone and
blushes with shame.

*

She is ashamed that someone sees she has just learned lute
and flute
Her finery retains the colors of an embroidery, this
elegant young girl is my neighbor.
Melancholy arises as soon as the lamp is lit in the cold,
facing shadows
Remote window, drinking as one pleases, alone singing of
spring.

QING DYNASTY
(1644–1911)

Wan Shu (1625–1688)

Wan Shu held a position as private secretary. He divided his energies between writing plays and composing poems to be sung, which was his great specialty. He left an original collection of forty diagrammatic poems entitled *Small Fragments of the Brocade of the Armillary Sphere* (*Xuanji cuijin*); the reference is familiar to us. I have extracted from it this labyrinth to be read in complex ways.

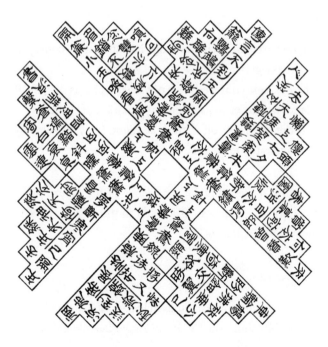

Figure 36.1 Wang Shu's Diagrammatic Poem

One hundred eighty-four characters here generate eight hepta-syllabic quatrains that are regular with respect to tonal alternation. In fact, eight heptasyllabic quatrains should require two hundred eighty characters. The method of reading involves reusing certain words. Moreover the characters are not all written in the same direction; the page must be turned several times. The title: "Mandarin Ducks, Heads Turned Round" is explained by the symmetrical arrangement at the center of the poem. The two characters that designate mandarin ducks, *yuan yang*, appear there eight times to be read in different directions. Mandarin ducks have a reputation for living as couples and being faithful. These eight poems give us their own version of the story of Su Hui.

Quatrain 1

To the parrot in a sculpted cage, it is difficult to convey a
     message
The message conveyed does not reach as far as the Jade Pass.
Mandarin ducks on a cushion, mandarin ducks dream
The dream breaks off in the cold night, (they are) already
     separated for years.

The parrot is a metaphor for a member of the literati gifted with great talents. The Jade Pass is located in the far west of China, at the end of the Great Wall.

Quatrain 2

Years go, years come, clothes in lively colors are faded
Wilted blossoms, their sight no longer bearable, when one
     leans by the gate.

Mandarin ducks on the loom, mandarin ducks in brocade
Brocade once woven, to hope to send it is difficult.

Quatrain 3

Out of anger the two eyebrows remain knit
Opening the blind, evening, a small jade (a beautiful
    woman) regards plum trees.
Mandarin ducks on the skirt, mandarin ducks
    embroidered
Embroidered so that the young man thus exclaims with
    admiration.

Quatrain 4

Coming before blossoms to admire spring at sunset
The spring garden dispels regrets, a hundred new blossoms.
Mandarin ducks on blossoms, fruits of mandarin ducks
In a fruit pit, two almonds, truly what cause to be angry!

The last line means: two women in the same heart.

Quatrain 5

Separation, weeping willows brush the inlaid carriage
Carriage wheels disappear from sight, leaning at the
    solitary village gate.
Mandarin ducks on letter paper, the characters of mandarin
    ducks
In each character we think of each other, the letter brings
    tears.

Quatrain 6

The letter is attached to the wild goose, conveyed by
    white clouds
Clouds follow one another, withered grass, darkness of
    falling dusk.
Mandarin ducks on the pond, the neck of mandarin ducks
At the time when necks want to be intertwined, wings are
    already separated.

Necks intertwined symbolizes physical union.

Quatrain 7

Autumn brings a slight chill to the weave of brocade
The weave is spread out, the weak one lies down there.
Mandarin ducks on the folding screen, painting of
    mandarin ducks
In the painting, two nest together, they seem to smile at people.

The expression "mandarin ducks nest together" evokes the couple
living under the same roof.

Quatrain 8

The man gone to the ends of the earth, the borders of
    heaven, calmly climbs the tower
High in the tower, evening of the seventh day of the
    seventh moon, contemplating the Herdsman
Mandarin ducks on the needle, thread of mandarin ducks
The thread waits to be tied, once again weak in autumn.

Another allusion to the legend of the Herdsman and the Weaver.

Zhang Yude (late 18th century)

Regarding Zhang Yude, we have only some idea of his era; we can guess that he was born between 1736 and 1796, and that he died between 1821 and 1851. A native of the present-day Shaanxi province, he may have stayed in Xi'an at the temple of the Little Goose Pagoda, hence the title of his collection: *Stelas of Reversible Poems on the Wild Goose Character from the Studio of Fragrant Snow* (*Xiangxuezhai yanzi huiwenshibei*). He composed twelve series with thirty poems each, for a total of three hundred sixty poems, which were engraved on twenty-four stelas five feet high by two feet wide. Only two hundred sixty poems remain intact in Daguan Lou, the Great Contemplation Pavilion, in the Hu district in southern Xi'an.

These are regular heptasyllabic octets, that is, they follow the rules of tonal alternation with flat pitch rhymes. Each series of poems exploits all the rhyme categories. Each poem is immediately followed by its reversal and whatever the reading direction, the rules of tonal alternation are always scrupulously respected.

Wild geese form characters, in the sky when they are flying, on the ground when they land. They migrate, make outward and return flights. The author establishes connections between the act of writing and reversible reading through their image. Writing, calligraphy, appears as the dominant theme in these poems. The author wrote the calligraphy for them himself, imitating the styles of some twenty famous works attributed to Wang Xizhi, Ouyang Xun, Yan Zhenqing, Liu Gongquan and others, nineteen calligraphers in all.

In the first poem, Zhang Yude begins by evoking the various stages in the invention of writing: knot in cords for representing ideas, the tracks of birds and animals that gave Cang Jie (an official close to the mythic Yellow Emperor) the idea for drawing the forms of objects, thus creating the first pictograms. The word *wen* 文 (text), had for its first meaning the "origin of forms."

Here is a print of the first poem in the collection (rhymes in *dong*) in the style of the ancient writings on bones and tortoise shells:

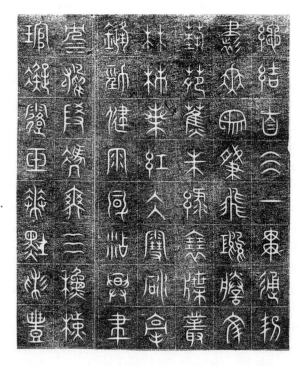

Figure 37.1 Zhang Yude's Poem set in Ancient Writing

Knots in a cord cross the sky
Engraved writing, suspended figures that wild geese in
    flight create.
Artistic collection of writings copied out, trunks of
    banana trees, green
Dense forest of strewn documents, leaves of persimmon
    trees, red.
Ice and snow sharpen hairs, tip robust and firm
Rain and wind add to the excitement, brush charged and
    energetic.
Hills in the pure autumn air, sleeves in the wind
Jade blossoms and stiffened dew, ink shimmering and
    glistening.

The second poem (rhymes in *zheng*) imitates the style of Ouyang
Xun and offers a reverse reading of the preceding one (Figure 37.2):

Glistening and shimmering the blossoms of ink, jade dew
    stiffens
Sleeves in the wind in the autumn air, high peaks are pure.
Energetic and deep handling of the brush is tied to wind
    and rain
Firm and robust tip sharpens snow and ice.
Forest of persimmon trees with red leaves, collected
    documents spread out
Collections of banana trees with green trunks, artistic
    writings copied.
Wild geese fly creating figures, engraved calligraphy in
    suspension
They cross the whole sky taking flight like knotted cords.

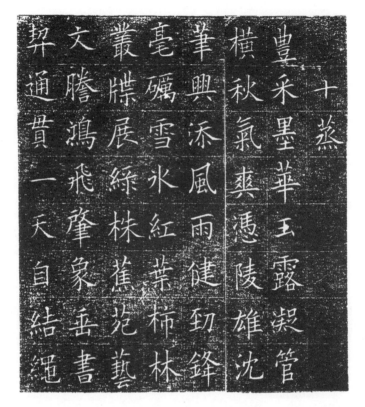

Figure 37.2 Calligraphy in the Style of Ouyang Xun

Calligraphers sometimes used a plant medium, such as banana leaves. In the second series, the ninth poem with rhymes in *wei*, calligraphy in the style of Wang Xizhi (Figure 37.3):

> Flat sand, the place of prints, they land there upon their return
> The words of wild geese begin the manuscript in a marvelous agitation.
> Oblique halo of ink that stretches away, calm wind

Cursive writing, well ordered, is reflected, bright snow.

A protective gauze over the painting, feathers hidden in the mist

Weaving the brocade, the shuttle turns like the brush's fine tip.

Multicolored clouds gather to form writing, bit by bit

Serpents and dragons make for the grass, trailing their banner.

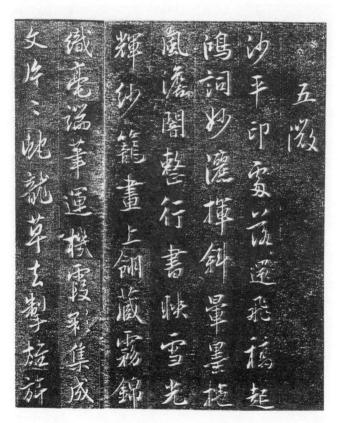

Figure 37.3 Calligraphy in the Style of Wang Xizhi

Inscriptions made directly on whitewashed walls were covered with a protective gauze. The mist hides the geese as the gauze did the painting. Grass lent its name to a writing style: wild-grass writing, which was very sinuous, hence the association with the movements of reptiles.

The following poem offers the reverse reading, with rhymes in *ma*, and calligraphy in the style of Ouyang Xun:

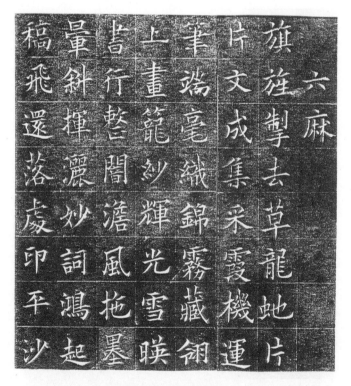

Figure 37.4 Calligraphy in the Style of Ouyang Xun

Trailing their banner, dragons and serpents in the grass
Bit by bit, the composed writing gathers multicolored
    clouds.
The shuttle is handled like the tip of a brush when
    weaving the brocade
Mist conceals feathers like gauze does a painting.
Bright, the snow reflects writing that continues, well
    ordered
Calm, the wind draws out the ink into an oblique halo.
Handling the brush with ease, marvelous words, wild
    geese begin their manuscript
Returning in flight to the place where they land, tracks on
    the flat sand.

An extract from the fourth series, the first poem, rhymes in *dong*,
with calligraphy in the style of Wang Xizhi (Figure 37.5):

The sky is cut with a track that crosses it from east to west
Wild geese play over the sea and dance in the blue-tinged
    azure.
Of their comings and goings, they record the stages by
    imprinting their tracks in snow
In heat and cold, they handle the squalls, from the brush is
    born the wind.
The whirling reaches its height, the text resembles the bird
Tail and head are linked, the tracks are like those of
    worms.
Carved into their marvelous coffer, ancient characters on
    the jade seal
Cleansed of the dust of the world, writing the banked
    clouds.

Figure 37.5 Calligraphy in the Style of Wang Xizhi

The reverse reading occurs in the following poem, with rhymes in *hui*. The calligraphy in the style of Pei Gongmei (Figure 37.6):

> Writing all the banked clouds cleanses away the world's
>   dust
> The jade coffer with characters of ancient seals is
>   marvelously carved.
> Worms make chains of tracks that go from head to tail
> Birds make manifest the text, they give form to the
>   whirling.

Wind gives birth to squalls under the brush, stirring heat
and cold

Snow imprints the stages by writing, noting the comings
and goings.

In blue-tinged azure, wild geese dance, they gather to play
over the sea

From east to west runs the track as soon as the sky opens.

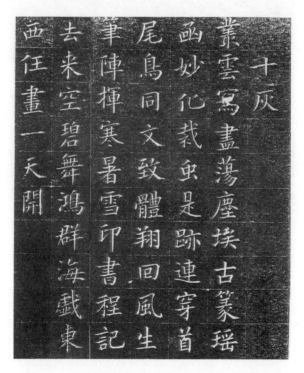

Figure 37.6 Calligraphy in the Style of Pei Gongmei

In the fourth series, this is the third poem, rhymes in *dong* and calligraphy in the style of Wang Xizhi:

Figure 37.7 Calligraphy in the Style of Wang Xizhi

Composition completed, the bird rises, feathers hide the tip
From the brush fall rain and dew in droplets, ground ink is
thick.
Traced lines cover the sky, distinguishing the wild from
the ordered
Shadow engulfs deep water, separating fish from dragon.

As far as immense and distant marches, transmitting the
　　letter on silk
On vast, flat sand, imprinting the seal with agility.
The bank of the Xiang sinks into autumn like a scroll
　　gently opening.
The sun follows the brush tip as the peak emerges from
　　clouds.

The reverse, rhymes in *yang,* and calligraphy in the style of Pei
Gongmei:

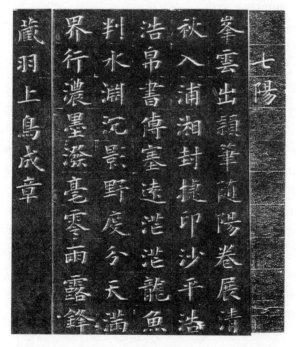

Figure 37.8 Calligraphy in the Style of Pei Gongmei

The summit reveals its peak through clouds, the brush
    follows the south-facing slope
The scroll unfurls in bright autumn as the Xiang flows
    between banks.
The seal is imprinted victoriously in the sand, peace is
    immense
The letter in silk is conveyed to distant and barren
    frontiers.
Dragons and fish cut through water in the darkness of the
    depths
The ordered and the wild separated in the sky by lines
    entirely traced.
The brush casts thick ink like the fine rain of dew
The tip is hidden in feathers, the bird completes the
    composition.

Beyond the many references to the history of calligraphy in these poems, Zhang Yude uses technical expressions, like the hidden tip or the impression of the seal. The "peak that pierces through clouds" is like the tip of the brush that must pierce through the paper, that is to say, it must be energetic.

Other reversible poems dating from the Qing dynasty have survived, but none of them equals this monumental collection, engraved in stone. Su Hui is present here through the evocation of the letter on silk, and wild geese etch into the sky the movements of reading. These two images have crossed the ages, conveying the Taoist theories of cosmology at the origin of the genre.

Return to the West

Regime changes, wars, revolutions—China's turbulent history in the twentieth century was hardly conducive to the transmission of the foundations of ancient thought. Reversible poems do not figure into recent official histories of Chinese literature. A few examples of circular poems sometimes appear in journals, under the rubric of games or curiosities.

It was much farther to the west, in the United States, that a significant new collection was published in 1978. Xiong Yinzuo, a Chinese emigrant, composed two hundred *Reversible Poems on the Four Seasons* in a highly classical style, accompanied by landscape paintings, followed by six hundred and four *Reversible Poems from the Ju Hsin Studio*, published in 1980. These texts enter into the philosophical tradition of the *I Ching*. They are devoted to the impressionistic notation of the smallest details of a landscape in order to comprehend the multiple changes at work in the universe, for which the reversible poem remains the most original poetic illustration.

And it was also from the other side of the Atlantic that I received a message a few years ago—an electronic message, not entrusted to wild geese. It came from an American poet and sinologist, David Hinton, who knew of my research into the matter of reversible poems. He himself was then working on a major anthology, *Classical Chinese Poetry*, in which he hoped to mention the work of Su Hui as I had reconstructed it. The "Map of the

Armillary Sphere" was reproduced in black and white in the "paper" version, but in color on the publisher's website. The reproduction was accompanied by a translation into English of one of the poem's four quadrants, following the division and configuration of the original. It is a true work of re-creation that resonates with his own poetic pursuits since David Hinton has himself experimented with new forms of textual spatialization. This is especially the case with *Fossil Sky*, which is presented as a folded geographic map and from which the text can be read starting from any point, turning the map-size sheet this way and that, following arabesques, contours of clouds in the sky or traces of birds in flight (see references in the bibliography). There is an astonishing convergence of interests across time, three continents and three languages. Seventeen centuries after the creation of Su Hui's poem, a new link is added to the chain of transmission, which is, as in the past, the work of an impassioned poet.

Although the colors of the "Map of the Armillary Sphere" were forgotten for many centuries, the readings they offer are now reconstructed. After long years of trying to understand their function, surmounting the difficulties of the ancient language, deciphering the poems, translating them, assembling other works in the same genre—now only this pleasure of transmitting and sharing them remains. About Su Hui's work, Empress Wu Zetian wrote nothing other than this in the year 692: "I have thus written these few notes to make it known to posterity."

Appendix:
The Ways of Reading Su Hui's Poem

Poems in Green: 3 Syllables

Upper right block

經離所懷歎嗟　　jing li suo huai tan jie
遐曠路傷中情　　xia kuang lu shang zhong qing
清幃房君無家　　qing wei fang jun wu jia
華飾容朗鏡明　　hua shi rong lang jing ming
英曜珠光紛葩　　ying yao zhu guang fen pa
多思感誰為榮　　duo si gan shui wei rong

<table>
<tr><td align="center">1st way:
12 lines of 3 syllables</td><td align="center">2nd way:
reverse of the previous</td></tr>
</table>

←———— 2 ←———— 1	11 ———→ 12 ———→
3 ———→ 4 ———→	←———— 10 ←———— 9
←———— 6 ←———— 5	7 ———→ 8 ———→
7 ———→ 8 ———→	←———— 6 ←———— 5
←———— 10 ←———— 9	3 ———→ 4 ———→
11 ———→ 12 ———→	←———— 2 ←———— 1

3rd way

4th way:
reverse of the previous

1 ⟶	2 ⟶	⟵ 12	⟵ 11
⟵ 4	⟵ 3	9 ⟶	10 ⟶
5 ⟶	6 ⟶	⟵ 8	⟵ 7
⟵ 8	⟵ 7	5 ⟶	6 ⟶
9 ⟶	10 ⟶	⟵ 4	⟵ 3
⟵ 12	⟵ 11	1 ⟶	2 ⟶

5th way

6th way:
reverse of the previous

⟵ 2	1 ⟶	⟵ 11	12 ⟶
⟵ 3	4 ⟶	⟵ 10	9 ⟶
⟵ 6	5 ⟶	⟵ 7	8 ⟶
⟵ 7	8 ⟶	⟵ 6	5 ⟶
⟵ 10	9 ⟶	⟵ 3	4 ⟶
⟵ 11	12 ⟶	⟵ 2	1 ⟶

7th way

8th way:
reverse of the previous

⟵ 1	2 ⟶	⟵ 12	11 ⟶
⟵ 4	3 ⟶	⟵ 9	10 ⟶
⟵ 5	6 ⟶	⟵ 8	7 ⟶
⟵ 8	7 ⟶	⟵ 5	6 ⟶
⟵ 9	10 ⟶	⟵ 4	3 ⟶
⟵ 12	11 ⟶	⟵ 1	2 ⟶

9th way:
middle right, 6 lines

← ——— 1
2 ———→
← ——— 3
4 ———→
← ——— 5
6 ———→

10th way:
reverse of the previous

6 ———→
← ——— 5
4 ———→
← ——— 3
2 ———→
← ——— 1

11th way:
middle left

1 ———→
2 ←———
3 ———→
4 ←———
5 ———→
← ——— 6

12th way:
reverse of the previous

6 ←———
5 ———→
← ——— 4
3 ———→
← ——— 2
1 ———→

13th way:
middle right

1 ———→
2 ———→
3 ———→
4 ———→
5 ———→
6 ———→

14th way:
reverse of the previous

6 ———→
5 ———→
4 ———→
3 ———→
2 ———→
1 ———→

15th way:
middle left, 6 lines

← 1

← 2

← 3

← 4

← 5

← 6

16th way:
reverse of the previous

← 6

← 5

← 4

← 3

← 2

← 1

17th way:
alternating left-right, 6 lines

← 1

← 2

← 3

← 4

← 5

← 6

18th way:
reverse of the previous

← 6

← 5

← 4

← 3

← 2

← 1

19th way:
alternating left-right, 6 lines

1 →

2 →

3 →

4 →

5 →

6 →

20th way: alternating
left-right from bottom

6 →

5 →

4 →

3 →

2 →

1 →

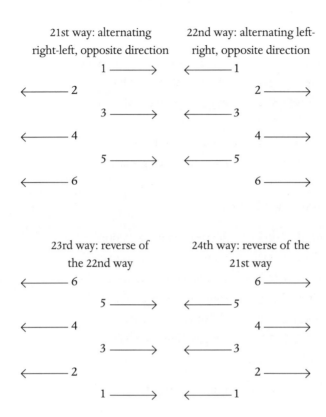

21st way: alternating
right-left, opposite direction

22nd way: alternating left-
right, opposite direction

23rd way: reverse of
the 22nd way

24th way: reverse of the
21st way

Identical ways of reading for the three following blocks:

Upper left block

廂東步階西遊	xiang dong bu jie xi you
休桃林陰翳桑	xiu tao lin yin yi sang
翔飛燕巢雙鳩	xiang fei yan chao shuang jiu
流泉清水激揚	liu quan qing shui ji yang
長君思悲好仇	chang jun si bei hao chou
愁歎發容摧傷	chou tan fa rong cui shang

Lower left block

微精感通明神	wei jing gan tong ming shen
雲浮寄身輕飛	yun fu ji shen qing fei
輝光飾粲殊文	hui guang shi can shu wen
群離散妾孤遺	qun li san qie gu yi
悲哀聲殊乖分	bei ai sheng shu guai fen
春傷應翔雁歸	chun shang ying xiang yan gui

Lower right block

滋愚讒浸頑凶	zi yu chan jin wan xiong
蒙謙退休孝慈	meng qian tui xiu xiao ci
疑危遠家和雍	yi wei yuan jia he yong
容節敦貞淑思	rong jie dun zhen shu si
持所貞記自慕	chi suo zhen ji zi mu
從是敬孝為基	cong shi jing xiao wei ji

Poems in Black: 6 Syllables

Upper double block

姿淑窈窕伯邵周風興自后妃
zi shu tiao yao bo shao zhou feng xing zi hou fei

歸思廣河女衞楚樊厲節中闈
gui si guang he nü wei chu fan li jie zhong wei

迆逶路遐志詠長歎不能奮飛
yi wei lu xia zhi yong chang tan bu neng fen fei

頎其人碩興齊雙發歌我袞衣

qi qi ren shuo xing qi shuang fa ge wo gun yi

蕤葳粲翠榮曜華觀冶容為誰

rui wei can cui rong yao hua guan ye rong wei shui

悲情我感傷情宮羽同聲相追

bei qing wo gan shang qing gong yu tong sheng xiang zhui

1st way: alternating
right-left, 6 lines of 6 syllables

1 ⟶

⟵ 2

3 ⟶

⟵ 4

5 ⟶

⟵ 6

2nd way: alternating
right-left from bottom, opposite
direction, 6 lines of 6 syllables

⟵ 6

5 ⟶

⟵ 4

3 ⟶

⟵ 2

1 ⟶

3rd way: alternating left-right,
opposite direction, 6 lines of
6 syllables

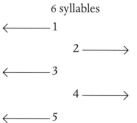

←——— 1

2 ———→

←——— 3

4 ———→

←——— 5

6 ———→

4th way: reverse reading
of the 1st way

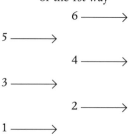

6 ———→

5 ———→

4 ———→

3 ———→

2 ———→

1 ———→

5th way: right block,
6 lines of 6 syllables

1 ———→

2 ———→

3 ———→

4 ———→

5 ———→

6 ———→

6th way: reverse of the previous,
     from bottom

6 ———→

5 ———→

4 ———→

3 ———→

2 ———→

1 ———→

7th way:
left block, 6 lines of 6 syllables

←——— 1

←——— 2

←——— 3

←——— 4

←——— 5

←——— 6

8th way:
from bottom

←——— 6

←——— 5

←——— 4

←——— 3

←——— 2

←——— 1

9th way: alternating right-left,
12 lines of 6 syllables

←——— 2   1 ———→

←——— 4   3 ———→

←——— 6   5 ———→

←——— 8   7 ———→

←——— 10   9 ———→

←——— 12 11 ———→

10th way:
reverse of the previous

←——— 11 12 ———→

←——— 9   10 ———→

←——— 7   8 ———→

←——— 5   6 ———→

←——— 3   4 ———→

←——— 1   2 ———→

11th way:
alternating left-right

←——— 1   2 ———→

←——— 3   4 ———→

←——— 5   6 ———→

←——— 7   8 ———→

←——— 9   10 ———→

←——— 11 12 ———→

12th way:
reverse of the previous

←———— 12   11 ————→

←———— 10   9 ————→

←———— 8   7 ————→

←———— 6   5 ————→

←———— 4   3 ————→

←———— 2   1 ————→

13th way: right-left by couplet,
12 lines of 6 syllables

←———— 3   1 ————→

←———— 4   2 ————→

←———— 7   5 ————→

←———— 8   6 ————→

←———— 11   9 ————→

←———— 12   10 ————→

14th way: alternating
left-right by couplet

←———— 1   3 ————→

←———— 2   4 ————→

←———— 5   7 ————→

←———— 6   8 ————→

←———— 9   11 ————→

←———— 10   12 ————→

15th way:

reverse of the previous

$\longleftarrow$ 12   10 $\longrightarrow$

$\longleftarrow$ 11   9 $\longrightarrow$

$\longleftarrow$ 8   6 $\longrightarrow$

$\longleftarrow$ 7   5 $\longrightarrow$

$\longleftarrow$ 4   2 $\longrightarrow$

$\longleftarrow$ 3   1 $\longrightarrow$

16th way:

reverse of the 13th way

$\longleftarrow$ 10   12 $\longrightarrow$

$\longleftarrow$ 9   11 $\longrightarrow$

$\longleftarrow$ 6   8 $\longrightarrow$

$\longleftarrow$ 5   7 $\longrightarrow$

$\longleftarrow$ 2   4 $\longrightarrow$

$\longleftarrow$ 1   3 $\longrightarrow$

Each of the four double blocks in black allow for the reading of 8 poems of 6 lines of 6 syllables, and 8 poems of 12 lines of 6 syllables, for a total of 64 poems. These blocks have different orientations, either horizontal, for the upper and lower double blocks, or vertical, for the left and right double blocks.

Left double block

禽心濱均深身	qin xin bin jun shen shen
伯改漢物日我	bo gai han wu ri wo
在者之品潤乎	zai zhe zhi pin run hu
誠惑步育浸集	jie huo bu yu jin ji
故暱飄施愆殃	gu ni piao shi qian yang
遺親飄生思愆	yi qin piao sheng si qian
廢遠微地積何	fei yuan wei di ji he
故離隔德怨因	gu li ge de yuan yin
君殊喬貴其備	jun shu qiao gui qi bei
子我木乎根嘗	zi wo mu hu gen chang
惟同誰均難苦	wei tong shui jun nan ku
新衾陰勻尋辛	xin qin yin yun xun xin

Right double block

形熒城榮明庭	xing ying cheng rong ming ting
未猶傾苟難闈	wei you qing gou nan wei
在炎在不受亂	zai yan zai bu shou luan
慎盛戒義消作	shen sheng jie yi xiao zuo
深興后姬原人	shen xing hou ji yuan ren
慮漸孽班禍讒	lü jian nie ban huo chan
察大趙婕所奸	cha da zhao jie suo jian
遠伐氏好恃凶	yuan fa shi yu shi xiong
禍用飛辭滋害	huo yong fei ci zi hai
在昭燕輦極我	zai zhao yan nian ji wo
防青實漢驕忠	fang qing shi han jiao zhong
萌青生成盈貞	meng qing sheng cheng ying zhen

Lower double block

馳若然條逝惟年殊白日西移
chi ruo ran tiao shi wei nian shu bai ri xi yi

虧不盈無衰必有衰無日不陂
kui bu ying wu shuai bi you shuai wu ri bu bei

離忠體一違心志殊憤激何施
li zhong ti yi wei xin zhi shu fen ji he shi

儀容仰俯榮華飭身將與誰為
yi rong yang fu rong hua chi shen jiang yu shui wei

眥何情憂感惟忘節上通神祇
zi he qing you gan wei wang jie shang tong shen shi

辭成者作體下葑菲采者無差
ci cheng zhe zuo ti xia feng fei cai zhe wu cha

Poems in Yellow: 5 Syllables

The four blocks in yellow each allow for a reading of 16 poems of 4 lines of 5 syllables, totaling 64 quatrains. Blocks from top to bottom are read horizontally, and those to right and left are read vertically. The same methods of reading alternating lines apply throughout.

Right block

仁顏貞寒	ren yan zhen han
賢喪物歲	xian sang wu sui
別改知識	bie gai zhi shi
行華終凋	xing hua zhong diao
士容始松	shi rong shi song

1st way: vertically from upper right

4	3	2	1
|	|	|	|
|	|	|	|
|	|	|	|

2nd way: right to left from bottom

|	|	|	|
|	|	|	|
|	|	|	|
4	3	2	1

3rd way: left to right from top

1	2	3	4
|	|	|	|
|	|	|	|
|	|	|	|

4th way: left to right from bottom

|	|	|	|
|	|	|	|
|	|	|	|
1	2	3	4

5th way: up and down from upper right

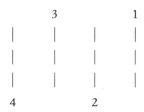

6th way: up and down from upper left

7th way: up and down from lower right

8th way: up and down from lower left

9th way: outside to inside from right

```
2       3       4       1
|       |       |       |
|       |       |       |
|       |       |       |
```

10th way: outside to inside from left

```
1       4       3       2
|       |       |       |
|       |       |       |
|       |       |       |
```

11th way: outside to inside from lower right

```
|       |       |       |
|       |       |       |
|       |       |       |
2       3       4       1
```

12th way: outside to inside from lower left

```
|       |       |       |
|       |       |       |
|       |       |       |
1       4       3       2
```

13th way: inside to outside from upper right

```
3     2     1     4
|     |     |     |
|     |     |     |
|     |     |     |
```

14th way: inside to outside from upper left

```
4     1     2     3
|     |     |     |
|     |     |     |
|     |     |     |
```

15th way: inside to outside from lower right

```
|     |     |     |
|     |     |     |
|     |     |     |
3     2     1     4
```

16th way: inside to outside from lower left

```
|     |     |     |
|     |     |     |
|     |     |     |
4     1     2     3
```

Left block

章時桑詩	zhang shi sang shi
微盛黳風	wei sheng yi feng
恨昭感興	hen zhao gan xing
微業孟鹿	wei ye meng lu
玄傾宣鳴	xuan qing xuan ming

Top block

藻文繁虎龍	zao wen fan hu long
榮曜華雕旂	rong yao hua diao qi
麗壯觀飾容	li zhuang guan shi rong
充顏曜繡衣	chong yan yao xiu yi

Bottom block

日往感年衰	ri wang gan nian shuai
思優遠勞情	si you yuan lao qing
慕歲殊歡時	mu sui shu tan shi
世異浮奇傾	shi yi fu qi qing

Central block

端無終始詩	duan wu zhong shi shi
此平始璇情	ci ping shi xuan qing
作蘇心璣明	zuo su xin ji ming
麗氏詩圖顯	li shi shi tu xian
辭理興義怨	ci li xing yi yuan

This block operates differently, since the 9 central characters and the 16 characters surrounding them must be considered separately.

Reading the perimeter generates 8 poems of 4 lines of 5 syllables. The last character of one line becomes the first character of the following line. Ways of reading consist of turning in one direction and then in the other, beginning from each of the fours sides successively.

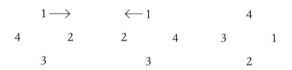

Poems in Purple: 4 Syllables

Each block allows for a reading of 10 quatrains in lines of 4 syllables.

Upper right block

寧自感思	ning zi gan si
孜孜傷情	zi zi shang qing
側君在時	ce jun zai shi
夢想勞形	meng xiang lao xing

1st way: horizontally from upper right, alternating directions

```
←——— 1
2 ———→
←——— 3
4 ———→
```

2nd way: reverse of the previous

4 ———→

←——— 3

2 ———→

←———1

3rd way: horizontally from upper left, left-right

1 ———→

2 ———→

3 ———→

4 ———→

4th way: reverse of the previous

4 ———→

3 ———→

2 ———→

1 ———→

5th way: outside to inside

1 ———→

4 ———→

3 ———→

2 ———→

6th way: reverse of the previous

2 ——————→
3 ——————→
4 ——————→
1 ——————→

7th way: inside to outside

4 ——————→
1 ——————→
2 ——————→
3 ——————→

8th way: reverse of the previous

3 ——————→
2 ——————→
1 ——————→
4 ——————→

9th way: by couplet

2 ——————→
1 ——————→
4 ——————→
3 ——————→

10th way: reverse of the previous

3 ⎯⎯→
4 ⎯⎯→
1 ⎯⎯→
2 ⎯⎯→

Upper left block

懷優是嬰	huai you shi ying
思何漫漫	si he man man
苦艱是丁	ku jian shi ding
我生何冤	wo sheng he yuan

Lower left block

悼思傷懷	dao si shang huai
歎永感悲	tan yong gan bei
戚戚情哀	qi qi qing ai
知我者誰	zhi wo zhe shui

Lower right block

念是舊愆	nian shi jiu qian
誰為獨居	shui wei du ju
賤女懷歎	jian nü huai tan
鄙賤何如	bi jian he ru

Poems in Red: 7 Syllables

These poems are located on the horizontal, vertical, and diagonal axes that represent the structure of the armillary sphere. There are 25 points of intersection, each of which corresponds to a rhyme word.

琴　秦　音　心　仁
qin qin yin xin ren

春　身　殷　欽　貞
chun shen yin qin zhen

新　神　心　深　臣
xin shen xin shen chen

純　麟　沉　林　倫
chun lin chen lin lun

親　人　身　民　津
qin ren shen min jin

The art of the combinatory clearly allows us to establish the exact number of readings ending in a rhyme word, but can we deduce from this the same number of poems? Although enjambment does not exist in Chinese poetry, the linking of lines requires a certain kind of compatibility in meaning. That is too subjective a criterion to allow for recourse to mathematics! According to the early authors, by moving around these various axes in straight lines, zigzags, and squares, it is possible to read 2848 quatrains. I will spare the reader the endless list of possibilities!

Selected Bibliography

WORKS IN WESTERN LANGUAGES

Boltz, Judith M. *A Survey of Taoist Literature: Tenth to Seventeenth Centuries.* Berkeley: Institute of East Asian Studies, University of California, 1987.

Cheng, François. *L'écriture poétique chinoise: suivi d'une anthologie des poèmes des T'ang.* Paris: Seuil, 1977. English edition: *Chinese Poetic Writing: With an Anthology of Tang Poetry.* Translated by Donald A. Riggs and Jerome P. Seaton. Bloomington: Indiana University Press, 1982.

Chow, Tse-tung. "Ancient Chinese Views on Literature, the Tao and their Relationships." *Chinese Literature: Essays, Articles, Reviews,* Vol. 1 , 1979.

Despeux, Catherine. *Traité d'alchimie et de physiologie taoïste.* Paris: Les Deux Océans, 1979.

_____. *Immortelles de la Chine ancienne: Taoïsme et alchimie féminine.* Paris: Puiseaux Pardès, 1990.

_____. *Taoïsme et corps humain: le Xiuzhentu.* Paris: Guy Trédaniel, 1994.

Drexler, Monika. *Daoistische Schriftmagie.* Stuttgart: Franze Steiner Verlag, 1994.

Granet, Marcel. *La pensée chinoise.* Paris: Albin Michel, 1968.

Hinton, David. *Fossil Sky.* New York: Archipelago Books, 2004.

_____. *Classical Chinese Poetry: An Anthology.* New York: Farrar, Straus and Giroux, 2008.

Ho, Peng Yoke. *The Astronomical Chapter of the Chin Shu.* The Hague: Mouton, 1966.

Jullien, François. *Figures de l'immanence: Pour une lecture philosophique des Yi king.* Paris: Grasset, 1993.

Kalinowski, Marc. "La transmission du dispositif des neuf palais sous les Six Dynasties," *Tantric and Taoist Studies in Honour of R. A. Stein,* edited by Michel Strickmann, Vol. 3, 1985.

_____. *Cosmologie et divination dans la Chine ancienne: Le compendium des cinq agents (Wuxing dayi, VIe siècle),* Paris: École Française d'Extrême-Orient, 1991.

Maspero, Henri. "Les instruments astronomiques des Chinois au temps des Han," *Mélanges chinois et bouddhiques*, Vol. 6, 1939.

_____. "Le Ming-t'ang et la crise religieuse chinoise avant les Han," *Mélanges chinois et bouddhiques*, Vol. 9, 1951.

_____. "L'astronomie chinoise avant les Han," *T'oung Pao*, 26, 1929.

Métail, Michèle. *La carte de la sphère armillaire de Su Hui, un poème chinois à lecture retournée du IV⁴ siècle.* Étais: Théatre Typographique, 1998.

_____. "Huiwenshi, poèmes chinois à lecture retournée," *Action Poétique*, No. 170, 2003.

Needham, Joseph. *Science and Civilization in China*, Vol. 3. Cambridge: Cambridge University Press, 1959.

Philastre, Paul-Louis-Félix. *Le Yi king, ou livre des changements de la dynastie des Tsheou*. Paris: A. Maisonneuve, 1982.

Reiter, Florian C. "Some Remarks on the Chinese Word *T'u* 'Chart, plan, design,'" *Oriens*, Vol. 32, 1990.

Robertson, Maureen A. "Periodization in the Arts and Patterns of Change in Traditional Chinese Literary History," in S. Bush and C. Murck, eds., *Theories of the Arts in China*. Princeton: Princeton University Press, 1983.

Robinet, Isabelle. "Le rôle et le sens des nombres dans la cosmologie et l'alchimie taoïstes," *Extrême-Orient Extrême-Occident*, Vol. 16, 1994.

WORKS IN CHINESE

Daozang. Wenwu chubanshe, Shanghai, 1987.

Fan Zhilin and Wu Gengshuo. *Quantangshi diangu cidian*. Hubei Cishu Chubanshe, 1989.

He Wenhui. "Huiwenshi kao," *Journal of Oriental Studies*, Vol. XIX, 1981.

_____. *Zatishi shili*. The Chinese University Press, Hong Kong, 1986.

Kang Wanmin. *Xuanjitu dufa*. Siku quanshu, jibu er, biejilei yi, jin.

Kong Guanglin. *Xuanjijin*.

Kong Pingzhong. *Qingjiang sandongji*.

Laozi. *Daodejing*.

Li Ruzhen. *Jinghuayuan*. Heluotushu chubanshe, Taipei, 1978.

Li Wei. *Shiyuan zhenpin, Xuanjitu*. Dongfang chubanshe, 1996.

Li Yu. *Hejing huiwenzhuan*. Chunfeng wenyi chubanshe, Shenyang, 1988.

Quantangshi. Zhonghua shuju. Beijing, 1985.

Quantangwen. Taipei, 1965.

Sang Shichang. *Huiwenleiju*. Siku quanshu, Jibu.

Shiyun xinbian peiwen shuyun daquan. Tianxia shuye yishu gongsi, Shanghai, 1965.

Su Zhecong. *Zhongguo lidai funü zuopinxuan*. Shanghai guji chubanshe, Shanghai, 1988.

Sun Zhensheng. *Yijing rumen*. Wenhua yishu chubanshe, Beijing, 1988.

Wan Shu. *Xuanji cuijin*.

Wang Jingni, Tang Qingmin, and Zheng Mengtong. *Hanwei liuchaoshi yishi*. Heilongjiang remnim chubanshe, Harbin, 1983.

Wang Yunxi and Gu Yisheng. *Weijin nanbeichao wenxue pipingshi*. Shanghai guji chubanshe, Shanghai, 1989.

Wang Zhonghou. *Miaojue shijie zhu huiwen wenxue*. Zhongguo xuehui, Xinjiapo, 1966.

Wei Gengyuan, Zhang Xinke, and Zhao Wangqin. *Xianqin han wei liuchaoshi jianshang cidian*. Sanqin chubanshe, Shanxi, 1990.

Weijin nanbeichao wenxueshi cankao ziliao. Zhonghua shuju, Beijing, 1962.

Wu Xiaoru, Wang Yunxi, and Luo Yuming. *Hanwei liuchaoshi jianshang cidian*. Shanghai cishu chubanshe, Shanghai, 1992.

Xu Hangsheng. *Weijin xuanxue shi*. Shanxi shifan daxue chubanshe, Xian, 1989.

Xu Shizeng. *Wenti mingbian xushuo*. Renmin Wenxue chubanshe, Beijing, 1962.

————. *Wenti mingbian*. Guangwen shuju, Taipei, 1972.

Zhang Yude. *Xiangxuezhai yanzi huiwenshibei*. Taiwan Shangwu yinshuguan, 1991.

Zheng Guangyi. *Zhongguo lidai cainü shigejianshang cidian*. Zhongguo gongren chubanshe, Beijing, 1991.

Zhongguo gudai tianwenxue chengjiu. Beijing Tianwenguan, 1987.

Zhongguo tianwenxue jianshi. Tianjin kexue jishu chubanshe, 1979.